Lincoln Christian College

Lincoln Christian College

Her childhood was spent
in Nazi Germany and Holland.
Her early youth—the days when
most girls are beginning to date—
was spent trying to survive
on tiny morsels of food while
in a concentration camp.
This is but the beginning
of the amazing story of
Dr. Vera Schlamm, the Jewish
pediatrician not a great deal
taller than some of her patients.
Her biography is the true
testimony of God's ability
to make "all things work
together for good."

# PURSUED

by Vera Schlamm
as told to Bob Friedman

A Division of G/L Publications
Glendale, California, U.S.A.

Bob Friedman graduated in journalism from San Diego State College. A newspaper reporter and free-lance writer, he has published magazine articles, books and frequently writes television scripts and screen plays. Like Vera Schlamm, Bob and his wife, Anita, are "completed Jews."

Scripture quoted is from the King James Version

© Copyright 1972 by G/L Publications
All rights reserved
Printed in U.S.A.
Second Printing, 1972

Published by
Regal Books Division, G/L Publications
Glendale, California 91209, U.S.A.

Library of Congress Catalog Card No. 72-77800
ISBN 0-8307-0153-2

# Contents

Baker & Taylor

46763

# Contents

CHAPTER ONE

# A Beautiful Start

My sister Marga thought I was stalling, but I really wasn't. I had heard enough to realize it wasn't something you just jump into. Having barely survived the constant calls of death from my past, I wanted my future life to generate from just the right place.

So I, Dr. Vera Schlamm, Jewish pediatrician not a great deal taller than some of my patients, began looking for a place to open my first private office.

I was enthused with many doctors in the Los Angeles area. But not quite enough. I waited patiently for the right situation to draw me quickly toward the right position. It was more like a slow pull than a fast tug.

A resident at Children's Hospital asked if I would fill in for him one day at a medical center in Glendale. I agreed, then found myself working with this private group of doctors twice a week. They added Tuesdays and Thursdays to my schedule, realizing I was only filling in temporarily until they could attract a pediatrician on a full-time basis.

They finally attracted me about January, 1960. It was a beautiful start. A ready-made practice, you might say, with children squirming on the chairs in the waiting room before meeting the new doctor.

Members of our group took turns being on call in the evenings, so often I would take my turn to thump, patch up or console adults. I didn't like this very much. When you're used to active, growing organisms it's hard to relate to someone who's already arrived! My colleagues viewed *my* patients with the same uneasiness. This was an exciting practice.

Soon February 28 came—and another birthday. Instead of a nicknack for the apartment or office, I asked Marga for an unusual present.

A Bible—with both Old and New Testaments. She had a whole Bible, so I figured I might as well get one too.

It was time to solidify my Judaism. Marga had read the Bible, and my brother-in-law Eric was finding it both fascinating and weird at the same time. He was surprised that Abraham could pass off his wife Sarah as his sister, and was shocked at some of the things Israel's great kings had done.

The more they talked, the more curious I became.

I was surrounded by thousands of so-called Christians, and felt it only fair I should know something of the New Testament. But not too much. It was the Old Testament, with its laws and prophets, which drew me like a spiritual magnet.

Marga had given me a standard King James Bible, with several colored pictures in it. I couldn't understand this. She obviously didn't realize I had no need of scenes depicting Jesus stilling a storm on the Sea of Galilee or Jesus raising up Peter's sick mother-in-law. She must have gone into a bookstore and asked for a Bible. Period. Marga couldn't have looked at it, or she would have known about the pictures. I was surprised to find it contained pictures of Jesus.

My reading began with Genesis, a logical start. I read and read, page after page, every once in a while sneaking a peek at the New Testament.

Each time I did this one of my former professor's sayings offered a satisfactory rationalization for my action. He used to say, "You can't go wrong if you're looking for the truth."

And I was.

I wasn't looking for anything in particular in the other Bible, the one with Matthew, for anyone would have to be crazy to think I even entertained the thought of becoming a Christian.

In my heart I felt the orthodox Jewish position was right, but I was unable to live up to its ideals and practices. I simply, but earnestly, wanted to be right with God.

I supplemented my Bible reading with weekly visits to Temple Emanuel on Friday nights. Before we all left for temple, I would stop by my parents' home and encourage them to say *kiddush*, a prayer for the Sabbath.

3

The rabbi's sermons were enjoyable, and so were the many verses of Scripture contained in our prayers. I was greatly impressed with what was carved over the entrance to the chapel in the temple: "And ye shall seek me, and find me, when ye shall search for me with all your heart" (Jeremiah 29:13).

My four-year-old niece Debbie wasn't searching for anything more than another cookie or two at the church-connected nursery school she was attending.

Yet she pulled an enthusiastic surprise on Marga when it was her turn to sing a song at the school's Mother's Day party. Ready? "Jesus Loves Me, This I Know!"

Marga just shrugged and said, "When she gets older and goes to temple she'll learn to sing 'Jesus Loves Me' in Hebrew."

My practice went smoothly as new patients were carried through the door or waddled in all by themselves. Then, on May 17, 1960, little Tommy was born.

I learned his birth date later when Lisa Palmer, his adoptive mother, called and asked if I would be Tommy's pediatrician. It seemed she wanted whoever was the group's pediatrician at the time. Very flattering.

We arranged for an appointment. I slowly hung up the phone and said to my nurse, "That sounded like a nice lady." It was something undefinable in her voice.

Mrs. Palmer brought both Tommy and her husband for the first visit. Immediately there was a softness, a soothing presence about them which made me at once both comfortable and intrigued.

Then I discovered that Milton Palmer, Tommy's proud "father," was in fact the *Reverend* Milton Palmer—assistant pastor of a Baptist church in Tujunga.

How very strange, I thought. I had taken care of several children belonging to ministers or missionaries, but their parents were nothing like these two.

I was drawn to Lisa. Her faith, the same heartfelt faith which had been so dramatic in my own life, was a daily reality for the Palmers.

She showed me a letter written in Tommy's baby book. It told of how they had tried to have a baby during fourteen years of marriage, but somehow it didn't seem to be God's will. They both knelt and prayed for their Lord to send them a little boy. Their prayer was answered in the form of a crying, healthy Tommy. I felt a kinship with them, for I could identify with anyone who really had faith.

In November of 1960, one year after I had begun my practice, I wrote out a request for my own chest X-ray at the office, grabbed the developed film and immediately concluded I had viral pneumonia, something that's difficult to treat very adequately.

I called my parents. They had always wanted to take care of me, so I told them now was their chance. "I'm very sick. Please do something." They arranged through their internist to have me admitted to St. John's Hospital in Santa Monica, then left soon afterwards for my nephew Peter's bar mitzvah in San Antonio.

My duties as a physician were temporarily halted as I assumed the role of a patient.

A week later my doctor told me he thought I had a

flare-up of tuberculosis which had haunted me in my youth. The thought of this not only frightened me but shoved memories back to a naked, crowded camp where TB rudely pushed helpless Jews across the delicate line from life to death.

I asked for a specialist, Dr. Joseph Boyle, who told me matter-of-factly that I should plan on going to a sanitarium. I accepted this. Acceptance is one virtue I had been forced to live with. My mental preparedness for a long rest in a sanitarium was tuned to a fine pitch.

It was almost a letdown when Dr. Boyle returned a week later to inform me a culture test had proven to be negative, and I didn't have TB after all.

I was quickly relieved.

I left the hospital with only one get-well card from any of my patients. It was from the Palmers.

Back to my office. Back to my apartment. Back to my Bible. I kept plowing through the Old Testament, skipping some repetitious parts in Chronicles and perhaps a few of the Psalms.

I reached Isaiah. We had studied him when I was in a Zionist youth group, so I knew he was one of our prophets. I obviously was on safe ground with whatever Isaiah had to say.

He had a lot to say. "Therefore the Lord himself shall give you a sign; Behold, a virgin shall conceive, and bear a son, and shall call his name Immanuel" (Isaiah 7:14).

A virgin? I was amazed! What was this word, used in this ridiculous context, doing in the Old Testament? Not that the idea of a virgin birth was a new concept to me. It wasn't. But in *Isaiah? My* Bible?

My periodic glances into the Gospel of Matthew, for the sake of academic curiosity, had familiarized me with certain aspects of the reported life of Christ. I had always told my gentile friends that we are all sons of God, and this Jesus wasn't any more of a son of God than I was a daughter of God!

Another verse jumped off the page at me. Isaiah 9:6: "For unto us a child is born, unto us a son is given: and the government shall be upon his shoulder: and his name shall be called Wonderful, Counsellor, The mighty God, The everlasting Father, The Prince of Peace."

Another verse talking about the son. I was fascinated, but this didn't help me solve my basic problem of authenticating my Judaism according to what *God* said.

Poring through the books of Moses and taking note of every law the Jews were commanded to follow, I soon gave up on the idea I could ever keep them all. Even though the Bible said, "Cursed *be* he that confirmeth not *all* the words of this law to do them" (Deuteronomy 27:26).

I knew different kinds of animal sacrifices were required, and this couldn't be done very well in my small apartment. Not that God would allow it if I could!

The many verses which said ". . . if you keep *all* my commandments" presented an uncomfortable obstacle in my quest for a happy relationship with God.

I had the same problem which troubled me as a child. How does one decide which laws he's going to keep? The Orthodox, Conservative and Reform Jews each adhere to different laws. But who are *we* to decide?

At least the Bible was showing me what the real laws were, and which were the traditional products of man's imagination.

During this time someone gave me *The Nun's Story* to read, and I soon felt a kinship with the heroine of the story. She, too, wanted to serve God the best way she knew how. She did this by joining a convent, but was frustrated by the number of man-made demands thrust upon her which she wanted to fulfill but couldn't. Her Mother Superior asked her to be humble enough to deliberately flunk an oral examination so another nun could go to the Congo as a nurse instead of her.

Stupid! That's not what God wants from us! This nun was constantly being asked to humble herself in an area that, to me, was not appropriate. I'm glad she finally broke down and gave the right answers at her examination.

I thought if I were to be a nun I'd be exactly like her.

*The Left Hand of God* was another book I read at this time, about a common man who assumed all the duties of a priest, pretending he was a clergyman. I decided his heart was probably more right with God than many actual priests.

Nuns, priests, rabbis, ministers—the whole religious structure swam in my head and finally settled into a somewhat confused tangle of heavenly inspiration and earthly public relations. Yet certain beliefs never faded from my previous training.

Such as my hope of the Messiah.

At Passover, celebrating the escape of the Jews from the hand of Pharaoh thousands of years ago, I would open the door of our home. For Elijah. The prophet who was to come and announce the arrival of the Messiah, our great King who would bring peace and defeat our enemies. This part of the ceremony was very real to me, and I actually expected our Messiah to come one year.

I continued searching and in the spring of 1961 my parents came to my place for our Passover *seder* (dinner). When the time came to open the door for Elijah, my mother said firmly, "Leave the chain on."

"How do you expect the Messiah to come in if the chain is on the door?" I asked.

We all broke out laughing. Even in our vague concept of the Messiah, and what He could do, we knew a chain wouldn't stop Him if He really wanted to come in!

But I felt if I'm going to open the door, I would open it all the way, not just a little bit. I kept waiting, each year, for Him to come.

He came. By way of Isaiah 53. And I couldn't handle it.

This entire Old Testament chapter was obviously talking about . . . no, it couldn't be. But the words, the descriptions, they pierced my heart and cried out "Yes, it *is*."

No question about it. It could apply to no one else. I slowly turned the page to the beginning, and once more read the words of Isaiah. A prophet studied by our Zionist youth group. A Jewish prophet. *My* prophet.

"Who hath believed our report?
And to whom is the arm of the LORD revealed?

"For he shall grow up before him as a tender plant,
and as a root out of a dry ground:
he hath no form nor comeliness;
and when we shall see him,
*there is* no beauty that we should desire him.

"He is despised and rejected of men;
a man of sorrows, and acquainted with grief:
and we hid as it were *our* faces from him;
he was despised, and we esteemed him not.

"Surely he hath borne our griefs,
and carried our sorrows:
yet we did esteem him stricken,
smitten of God, and afflicted.

"But he *was* wounded for our transgressions,
*he was* bruised for our iniquities:
the chastisement of our peace *was* upon him;
and with his stripes we are healed.

"All we like sheep have gone astray;
we have turned every one to his own way;
and the LORD hath laid on him
the iniquity of us all.

"He was oppressed, and he was afflicted,
yet he opened not his mouth:
he is brought as a lamb to the slaughter,
and as a sheep before her shearers is dumb,
so he openeth not his mouth.

"He was taken from prison and from judgment:

and who shall declare his generation?
for he was cut off out of the land of the living:
for the transgression of my people was he stricken.

"And he made his grave with the wicked,
and with the rich in his death;
because he had done no violence,
neither *was any* deceit in his mouth.

"Yet it pleased the LORD to bruise him;
he hath put *him* to grief:

"when thou shalt make his soul an offering for sin,
he shall see *his* seed,
he shall prolong *his* days,
and the pleasure of the LORD shall prosper in his
hand.

"He shall see the travail of his soul,
*and* shall be satisfied:
by his knowledge shall my righteous servant justify
many;
for he shall bear their iniquities.

"Therefore will I divide him *a portion* with the great,
and he shall divide the spoil with the strong;
because he hath poured out his soul unto death:
and he was numbered with the transgressors;
and he bare the sin of many,
and made intercession for the transgressors."

My own soul was tormented by the conclusion of
this passage. The consequences I wouldn't consider.
Then, in the midst of my own confusion, a happy
thought struck me. I was reading the King James
Version! A Protestant Bible! Of course, it was

slanted to sound that way. I went to sleep on this Tuesday night, confident I had caught the gentiles at a not-too-clever trick.

Friday night I eagerly went to services at temple, snatched up a solid, legitimate *Jewish* Bible from in front of my seat and anxiously turned to Isaiah 53. It was basically the same message. A few minor words changed. The "trick" backfired. I experimented by showing the passage to my father. I trusted that if he read it he would see the same things I had seen. He didn't have the faintest idea what I was showing him.

I recalled a passage from Isaiah, quoted by Jesus in one of my quick trips into Matthew, in which Isaiah says, "Also I heard the voice of the Lord, saying, Whom shall I send, and who will go for us? Then said I, Here am I; send me.

"And he said, Go, and tell this people, Hear ye indeed, but understand not; and see ye indeed, but perceive not" (Isaiah 6:8,9. Also see Matthew 13:14, 15).

All of a sudden I saw, but didn't know what to do with what I perceived.

Jesus was as foreign to me as a cartoon of an invading Martian. But at least I treated the Martian with neutrality. As for this Jesus, I was raised with an uneasiness about Him I didn't understand.

I only knew I had swallowed giant amounts of an animalistic state of being created by smirking men whom I thought represented this same Jesus. All gentiles. All Christians. From the barbed wire to the gas chambers.

No, something was wrong. Somewhere. I'd find

where the flaws were that would crack to pieces what Isaiah teased me with. It had to be.

I knew I would be an absolute traitor to the Jewish people if I believed in Jesus.

# CHAPTER TWO

# Strands of a Web

I was born February 28, 1923 in Berlin, Germany.
When I was one year old severe eczema hospitalized
me for several days until my parents decided to take
me home. Doctors had given me a fifty percent
chance of living. Immediately I demanded two bottles at each feeding to satisfy my appetite, so obviously I gave myself better odds than the doctors had!

My parents' first child died at the age of six weeks;
then my older sister, Marga, and I were born two
years apart.

My father, Max, manufactured dresses and
blouses—wholesale ladies' wear—a typical Jewish
occupation and quite satisfactory. My mother, Meta,
assisted him with about fifty employees.

Because of my frail nature and sickness a private

nurse came to live with us for two years. She would help in my bedtime routine. I'd lie in the crib, thrust my hands out to the side and watch them be tied firmly to the wooden slats. No hands, no scratching. Standard operating procedure.

I didn't resent this, for I knew it was for my own good. As I waited for sleep to take my mind away from this uncomfortable position I would say a little prayer. I believe the nurse taught it to me.

"I am small, my heart is clean, no one should live in it but God alone."

At three or four years of age I meant it. I thought about what I was saying, and knew I *was* little, I *was* clean and I really didn't want anyone to live in my heart but God.

Later I learned another prayer which went something like: "I go to bed now, close my eyes, and may the angels watch over me." Soon I also could recite the *schmah* (Deuteronomy 6:4-6).

I developed into an active, healthy girl who stood somewhat shorter than my peers. Our dolls were smaller than me, though, and Marga and I would pretend they had to go to school. We even had books for them.

Marga was a good leader and I was a natural follower, so we got along well together. I usually did what she told me to do and we shared everything. Like the measles. Which caused me to miss my first day of school, something I had been dreaming about for years. It took me the longest time to forgive Marga for that, for I knew on the first day the children played, with a minimum of work!

As a tiny six-year-old I bounded into the school

office to be assigned to class and was met with my first inkling of an attitude which would haunt me time and time again. The principal had somehow concluded my intelligence was directly proportional to my height. And my, was I short! He made me recite a poem, which I did, and I ended it with a gesture demanded by the lyric—I stuck my tongue out at him! He admitted me to class.

We lived in a nicely furnished apartment, for in those days only the very rich could afford a single residence—which usually came in the form of a villa. On some Sundays the family would go to the cemetery where mother and father visited their parents' graves. I had always felt an affinity for my sister who had died as a baby, so I would wander over to where she was buried. I wondered what death was all about.

We lit the candles Friday night and said the blessing over the wine. My parents occasionally talked about God, but not in a way which would give me an insight as to His nature.

Relatives visited for Sabbath or else came over during the High Holidays or for Passover in the spring. Passover marked a time when the entire family would congregate for a seder at our home.

I took Passover very seriously, and was impressed that the angel of death passed over the Jewish homes where the blood had been marked on the doorposts and thereby saved the firstborn. Did he pass over because the residents were Jewish, or because the blood was on the outside? I was curious about the Egyptians. Would the blood have saved *their* firstborn?

In temple I reverently recited the prayers, and was sincere about each one.

17

For an hour, two or three times a week, each student in public school would attend a Catholic, Protestant or Jewish class for religious training.

Besides a little Hebrew, we learned about the history of Israel and of Judah—the northern and southern kingdoms. Israel was captured by the Assyrians well before Judah was taken by Babylon. God had protected the ones who believed in Him, Judah, but then they, too, fell away.

We were instructed in all of the famous stories of Genesis and Exodus. Abraham, Isaac and Jacob. Joseph and his interpretations of dreams. Solomon's wisdom.

My unbreakable bond with Old Testament Jews was not affected by the Christmas carols the entire school sang in December. This was no big thing, actually, and we rather enjoyed it. Even my parents had a Christmas tree for the benefit of our gentile housekeeper. We gave her a present on Christmas day, but opened our own presents during Chanukah. I was proud of the way the Maccabees had bravely defeated the tyrants persecuting the Jews.

I was ten years old when Hitler came into power.

My father was reading the paper in bed when it announced Hitler's political victory, and he just shook his head and said, "This isn't good for the Jews." Perhaps this is the first time I had heard *der Führer's* name.

The impact of what was happening hit me directly through my friends a short time later. Rosemarie, a gentile friend all the way through grade school, would share secrets with me and we constantly played together. I also would go around with Marion, a Jewish girl who had the nicest birthday parties at her home. As soon as the hate propaganda began in school Rosemarie snubbed me.

A new class in national socialism created two major problems at school. First, it taught the gentile students to despise the Jews. Second, during the hour when the gentile minds were being warped toward a solid anti-Semitic contempt, the Jewish students had free time—which enraged the gentiles. Yet we Jewish children would rather have been in class, because we felt very much out of it.

There also were "optional" sports activities after classes which the gentiles were greatly encouraged to attend and the Jews were forbidden to participate in. They didn't like being forced to go, and we didn't like not being able to go.

Often a teacher would announce Jewish children couldn't do one thing or another. No explanation was necessary, for by now everyone knew Jews were to be hated and were no part of nationalistic Germany.

They were much more sophisticated in Marga's class. Soon the gentiles wouldn't sit near the Jewish students nor hang their coats next to "Jewish" coats for fear of "contamination".

My parents spent long hours working and seldom commented on the situation. One of my father's employees, a member of the SS, tried to make trouble for him. Yet many friends would say, "Oh, don't leave Germany, Mr. Schlamm, because you know this will be over in a little while. Don't be frightened away!"

The smartest thing we could have done at that

point was to leave, but business picked up and we stayed. Many German Jews considered themselves Germans first and Jews second. I screamed just as loudly as the gentiles did when we heard at school that Germany had taken back a part of France she lost after World War I. This was 1933.

In 1935 the pressure increased to such a degree that Marga and I were taken out of public school by our parents and placed in an exclusively Jewish school. I was twelve and Marga fourteen. I felt very uneasy going to a new school with strange children there staring at Jutta Vera Schlamm, the freshly arrived midget. The first time our music teacher looked at me he broke out into hysterical laughter because of my height. Extremely rude—and I'm not even four feet nine as an adult!

In the summer of 1936 a boy told a very dirty poem to a group of us. I didn't understand it. My parents were of no help after I repeated it to them for they sharply warned me not to mention it to anyone. No explanation, just warnings.

That fall I was sent to a school near Merano, Italy. Miserable. Depressing. Frustrating. There were no children of my own age there, and consequently the wrong classes were offered. I either had to jump a year, which would have placed me into a number of "second-year" courses of which I lacked the first year, or else I had to fall back. A few years before I had had an opportunity to skip a class, but my parents refused permission. If they had only said yes I would have . . . oh, what's the use. I fell back.

My dormant curiosity came back to life and I wondered about something. That poem. That dirty poem whose meaning I still wasn't sure of. I asked my friends at school about it, and soon I had established a reputation for myself of spreading horrible ideas and being, therefore, a rotten child.

I wasn't allowed to speak to anyone for three days. Yet I finally began to understand the poem and what sex involved. The shock of this revelation forced me to exclaim; "Oh! My parents would never do anything like that! Could it really be? Is that the way it is?" I was simply curious. Not rotten.

In spite of what was being said about me, I prayed to God for His forgiveness if I had done anything wrong. I was in bed, and soon a perfect peace came over me and I knew I was all right with God. It no longer mattered what the others thought.

To keep in touch with home I wrote to Marion as well as my family. Then, as a special treat, Marga came to visit for a while. I enjoyed the mountains of Italy, the beauty of sparkling streams and good food, but the school itself ruined many things for me.

My piano teacher was so incompetent I stopped taking lessons begun in Berlin. Her husband was my Latin teacher—and extremely cruel. He'd force me to repeat grammatical exercises over and over, never telling me if I was correct or not. He'd just say "repeat" again and again.

Even if you knew the material at the start you weren't certain of your sanity at the end. "Repeat." "Repeat." "Repeat." He drove me crazy.

His nastiness reached a peak when he teased me about being so short. He was much worse than the students. This man also managed to ruin my love of skiing, as he would throw me down in the snow for the "fun of it." I was a good sport, but after a while I stopped laughing.

He was a German gentile and, I believe, not too crazy about my people. His hostile attitude turned out to be but the first few strands of a growing web of persecution waiting for me upon my return to Berlin.

# CHAPTER THREE

# Heat-up to a Fast Boil

I was fourteen when I returned to my own school and at once banged my head against a social wall of typical junior high school cliques. The headaches I received were fierce. Literally. One headache after another. Psychological, I'm sure, but at the time they were real enough for me to miss most of my classes. I had been an A-plus student before, but my marks were speedily dropping to Cs and Ds.

Mornings began with a touch of excitement. I was always the punctual one, whereas Marga just barely managed to appear in the nick of time. I'd leave before my sister in the mornings and walk to the streetcar stop. As Marga ran through the front door our housekeeper would shove coffee and a roll with butter and jam at her. She tried to drink and eat while sprinting toward the corner. We had special signals prepared, so if I saw the streetcar coming I'd tell her to rush. If there was time, she'd slow down. Most mornings she ran.

One afternoon Marion and I rode our bicycles to a little plaza a few blocks away where we rode around and around in a dizzy circle. When I returned home the whole house was in an uproar. Our Doberman pinscher had followed me without my knowing it and was lost. Marga and I didn't sleep much that night, and the next morning we made a futile attempt to beg off going to school. That afternoon I made an excuse that I had a headache and was in such bad shape Marga would just *have* to help me home. We ran most of the way. As we burst through the door the Doberman pinscher was waiting for us. Someone had brought him back.

It was 1938. My parents had already applied to both Holland and the United States for visas. They knew we wouldn't be able to stay in Germany for long. Because of this, and my chronic emotional problem, I quit school.

I left in April at the end of the school year, having completed the ninth grade and quite determined never, never, to return to a formal academic life. My time became filled with shorthand and typing lessons in the day and a course in intensive Spanish in the evenings, taught by a Jewish agency. I enjoyed this immensely, giving my ego a much-needed boost by tutoring a sixty-year-old man having trouble with our lessons.

At that time we had a gentile neighbor named Alfred. His parents and mine promoted our friendship, although neither one of us was exactly thrilled by the idea. For about six months we played or rode our bicycles together until the day came when Alfred realized it wasn't the ideal thing for him to do—ride with a Jewish girl. We stopped seeing each other.

Meanwhile, father had established a branch of his business in Amsterdam and during his many train rides to Holland had become good friends with one of the Pullman porters.

This man had a home in the suburbs right outside of Berlin. I spent quite a few weekends with his family in order to escape the persecution which was rapidly heating up from a steady simmer to a fast boil. None of his neighbors were allowed to know I was Jewish. My light blond hair and gentile features eased me nicely out of a stereotype "Jewish look" into a well-bred member of the "Aryan" race. We'd go for a walk and someone would stop us and say, "What a pretty German girl! So typically Germanic!"

I smiled.

The porter's daughter and son-in-law lived with them. One day a relative of the younger man came to visit and eyed me suspiciously. He was a member of the SS and, true to form, asked who I was.

"That's my daughter!" the younger woman said.

"You don't have a daughter!"

He had been there five years before and didn't recall seeing a daughter. She explained on that occasion her mother had taken me to town and he had missed me. He didn't buy the story.

27

"Can't you see it?" the SS man's wife interrupted, "she's just exactly like her mother!" I smiled. The wife used a German expression which, translated, means "cut out of her face."

After that I called them mother, father, grandmother and grandfather. It was a big game and, at fifteen, I passed for a seven-year-old.

Which presented a problem. A seven-year-old doesn't announce she's going to sit down and read a book, which I wanted to do. I "shyly" walked in and approached my "mother" to show her a volume.

"Mother," I began softly, "are there pictures in this book?"

"Yes, dear."

"May I look at them?"

"Yes."

So I sat on the couch and read my book. Terribly clever, I thought.

About this time my favorite cousin, Guenther, came to visit us in Berlin from his country home. He was attending a carpentry school, one of many trade centers designed to teach Jewish youth skills before they left for Palestine. We knew Palestine couldn't exist with every person a businessman!

When he first arrived to spend a weekend Marga and I were struck with both amusement and embarrassment. The boy from the country was dressed like a bumpkin, with an ill-fitting suit and ridiculous hat. Marga and I were told we had to introduce him to our friends. Fortunately father bought him a new suit and hat. Guenther was six months older than I. We did have good times together and could still go to the theater and different public places. Near the end of his stay his parents came to visit. And when his parents came, the whole *mishpucha* (family) came.

The chatter of all our relatives in the small apartment was as thick as the billows of curling smoke from their cigarettes. Guenther offered to take me for a walk to temporarily flee the noise and stale air. I said fine and we slipped out unnoticed.

We could enjoy each other's company by simply strolling past store windows and observing the large Saturday night crowds swarming over the streets. We came to a landmark, a memorial church for Kaiser Wilhelm, which usually takes twenty minutes to walk to.

We had been gone an hour. My light summer dress did nothing to keep off the chilly night air. We saw a movie house, off limits for Jews, and stared at each other. Should we?

We did. It was warm inside and after a few minutes danger motivated me more than warmth and we left. Guenther and I zigzagged through the crowd and as we raced home I remembered a nickel bet I had recently lost to him.

"Hey, Guenther, I'll bet you a nickel we're going to get into trouble at home!"

"Why should we get into trouble? We didn't do anything."

We came into the living room and confronted our fathers. For the first time I realized how much these brothers looked alike. Lips clamped. Eyes narrowed. Brows wrinkled.

"Where have you been?"

They thought we had stayed at a local ice-cream parlor where the soldiers often went in and rounded up all the Jews. It wasn't very safe to be on the streets alone. At once I looked at Guenther.

"I won!"

That took the edge off it. We finally convinced our parents we had not stayed in the ice-cream parlor— although we *did* get an ice cream and left right away. We were smart enough not to try anything really wrong.

That year, 1938, two of my uncles left Germany. Another aunt and uncle whom I didn't know very well had already left for Brazil three years earlier. They wrote and said they were poor, unhappy and used boxes for furniture.

They begged us to leave, for they knew more about what was happening in Germany than we did.

Marga and I used to take care of our cousins who left in 1938. They boarded the streetcar after we did on the way to the Jewish school and got off before us on the way home. We checked to make sure they were all right and often played together after classes.

Father went on what I thought was another business trip October 12. The following days were strange, with mother and Marga always leaving me to see the lawyers in an attempt to free my uncle from prison. They said he had been involved in an attempt to smuggle his own money into Holland.

*November 9, 1938.* The German soldiers collected thousands of Jewish men and herded them into concentration camps for a series of horrible tortures. I nervously asked my mother if father had escaped this while in Holland.

Yes, he was safe, she said. But not in Holland. For the past month he had been in prison.

# CHAPTER FOUR

# Sign of the White Carnation

Father had tried to smuggle his own money out of the country with a man traveling from Germany to Holland. All of our private funds had been confiscated. When you left Germany, you left everything. He wanted to have a few marks waiting for us if we made it to Holland.

The Germans found my father's name and address in the man's pocket and picked father up. At this time it was an honor and not a disgrace for a Jewish man to be imprisoned.

Then rumors circulated that a young Jewish boy had killed a German. Supposedly, this led to the violent mob reaction which roared through the city on November 9, 1938.

*November 9.* The day they burned all the synagogues. And Jewish centers. And every business with a "JEWISH STORE" sign in the window. Screaming, fiercely yelling out anti-Semitic slogans, the gentile civilians made it a real family affair. Including my former playmate, Alfred!

A highly organized mass of adults and youth threw bricks, stones, chunks of pavement—anything—through windows, at well-stocked shelves and trembling owners. They were very thorough. It went on for a good twenty-four hours. I huddled in our apartment and listened to hundreds of bottles being smashed at the corner drugstore. We could hear everything from where we lived and my imagination soon filled in details of unseen destruction.

My mother was away with Marga when it started. I paced along a thin path stomped into the rug. Back and forth, back and forth. Emmi, our housekeeper, accused me of imitating a lion in a cage. It was really happening. There was nothing you could do about it. Nervously I feared something terrible had happened to mother. Later, a turn of the front door knob—and I knew mother was safe.

The shock of this unexpected attack was not as great as the sinking feeling which numbed the merchants as they helplessly watched a life's work being systematically destroyed. You couldn't resist. You couldn't fight. You couldn't get help.

If we had lived in a ghetto like Warsaw perhaps we could have mustered strength as a unit. But we were too scattered for that in Berlin. We were easily divided and conquered. The sadness hit me immediately when I went outside the next day after most of the mob had dispersed.

I was walking briskly to an English lesson when I passed the drugstore. For a fraction of a second I glanced at the owner's face as he stared with blank eyes at children tossing in a few more rocks for good measure. I'll never forget it.

Utter helplessness. Agony brought to a sharp peak and then leveling off into a narrow road which leads to no future but which you must keep moving upon. No recourse. No police protection. No civilian help. The entire world against you, and you but half a man.

Mother promptly sold our furniture, pictures and anything else which would raise money for our illegal passage into Holland. We needed several thousand dollars. The money was finally collected and arrangements made with those men now in this type of business.

Wednesday, December 1, 1938, father was released on parole with instructions to report to his board the following Monday. Trouble was already gathering momentum for the weekend when we heard another wave of persecution would hit the Jews.

We told Emmi we would be gone for a couple of days. We were not worried about her telling on us, for she was a dear friend, but it was better she didn't know for her own protection. Later, when she was questioned, she could honestly say she didn't know we were leaving.

Emmi, in a demonstration of loyalty to our family, would rip apart the many summonses she received to attend nationalistic meetings. Before we left she came to me and said, "Please, you aren't going to leave without telling me, are you?"

Thursday I was told we would be trying to go across the border and to take anything I wished. The entire idea of this type of adventure tickled my fifteen-year-old fancy. It was very exciting.

At once I dug deep into a pile of family photographs and began to pick the ones I liked best. My parents wondered how, of all things, I could choose photographs. But over the years they were very grateful.

Friday morning I called Marion. I was a perfect actress as I casually said I wanted to know how she was and so forth. No one was permitted to know of our plans, yet I didn't want Marion to say I never called.

Friday afternoon, luggage in hand, we left our apartment and walked down the street. A few blocks passed under foot before a car pulled to the side and picked us up. Driving all day, becoming lost in a strange mixture of anxiety and hope, we finally reached the border town of Aachen at midnight.

It was too late to make an attempt that night. We sneaked to the rear of an inn and tiptoed to a few rooms in the back. Up front, in the restaurant, German soldiers were loudly drinking and laughing away the evening.

Late the next afternoon we boarded a train at a small station, with instructions to get off at a tiny community where a man wearing a white carnation in his lapel would meet us. Television drama takes a poor second to real life circumstances.

He was waiting. We all piled into his car and as he drove he explained a play-by-play plan of what we were to do at a remote soccer field.

The night became deadly black with no lights or stars to illumine our path. We quietly stopped the car at this open field located in swampy country directly on the German-Holland border.

He pointed to a near set of goal posts. Our starting point. Then his finger stretched a little and indicated another set of posts across the field—not quite as far apart as those on an American football gridiron. Our finishing point.

We merely had to run from one set of goals across the field to the other and wait for a Dutchman to go "tch, tch, tch" in the night. At this point we'd slip into Holland and the whole family would have scored.

Somehow the other side missed the point. We grabbed our things and sloshed across the field, waiting patiently under the far posts, straining our ears for the sound of "tch, tch, tch."

It never came. We were severely warned not to try to make it by ourselves, for the swamps were extremely dangerous. The driver advised us to simply wait.

Which we did. Minute after painful minute. We stood facing each other, mother and father, Marga and myself. The driver had also instructed us what to say in case we were caught so he wouldn't get into trouble. He assured us it was "99 percent" safe.

Standing there in the freezing night I kept dwelling on that one percent he hadn't included. A good *yiddisha* mind.

For two hours we didn't say a word and subdued our breathing to minimum volume. We hid our faces as much as possible so a passing patrol wouldn't throw any light off of our shiny skin.

As soon as my feet were planted in a semi-permanent position I began to pray. I continued the entire time in prayer, silently, strictly between me and God.

I promised God everything under the sun if He'd somehow get us out. For years my parents had taken me from one doctor to the next in a vain attempt to help me grow. I told God I didn't care anymore if I grew—just so we'd be free. (This was very important and for years afterwards I was hesitant about seeing a doctor for fear I would be breaking my promise to God.)

I finally whispered to father, begging him to return to Germany.

"It's better to be in Germany, and healthy, than in Holland with pneumonia!"

"Shhh!"

I really didn't understand the circumstances, of course. Cold and hunger had taken the sharpness from my reasoning powers. I simply knew I was miserable with nowhere to go.

At last father decided to go back. No one was going to come for us. Our legs ached as we headed through the rain toward the other side of the field. Then . . .

"Stop or I'll shoot!"

The heavy voice stabbed the silence of the night and pierced the eerie quietness. What was happening? Caught? *Hey, father! Father!*

He started running. What could he be thinking? Trying to outrace a bullet? Once more the voice cried out.

"Stop or I'll shoot!"

"Father, come back! Father, don't . . . come back!" We screamed after him and he stopped in his tracks, slowly turned and walked back to his family. We searched each other's faces before peering up at our captor.

It was the Gestapo.

# CHAPTER FIVE

# Aachen, Amsterdam

I held my father's hand and Marga held mother's. He was shaking violently from our sudden arrest and from the possibilities of what might happen to him if they discovered he was on parole. I put my lips next to his ear.

"Father, don't worry, God is going to get us out of this."

I meant it. I believed it.

At Gestapo headquarters they took the women into a little room and forced us to strip. Marga became very deliberate about removing one piece of clothing after another and occasionally exchanged glances with me.

41

She had been entrusted with father's parole slip which he needed at the border to convince the Dutch how important it was they let him in. Marga had hidden it where girls hide things. Just as she had undressed down to her underwear, and could afford to go no further, she calmly looked at the woman guard.

"I have some dry stockings in my luggage in the other room. Would you mind getting them?"

It was a miracle. The woman agreed. In her absence Marga hurriedly got dressed again and when the guard returned she never complained. She had seen Marga that far, so what else was there? Only the parole slip—and it was safe.

My mother, sister and I had valid passports and exit visas. The Gestapo said they would let us go. At this point they were still willing to let the Jews leave Germany, but because of father's situation we couldn't take advantage of it.

Father's passport was taken when he was in prison. He had only ten dollars on him, the limit one could carry, and no personal belongings or papers. The women had suitcases.

We told them he was merely escorting us to the border with obviously no plans of going across himself. Then, in his frantic excitement, father blurted out:

"Well, I have to be back in Berlin on Monday anyway. I have to be back on Monday!"

We all cringed for we thought the next minute he'd mention he had to report to the police! Why couldn't he have just stuck to the first story? We constantly interrupted to stop him from committing a fatal error. At one point he almost said it.

They didn't want to let father go until Marga pleaded with them, suggesting they call one of their most trusted men to drive us all back to the train station and make sure we were on our way to Berlin.

We had agreed we would all go back to Berlin rather than ride across the border and leave father with the Gestapo. The Gestapo hadn't exactly established a reputation for reasoning with Jewish people.

Marga's suggestion was accepted—on the condition a quick call to Berlin confirmed our story.

That would have undone us right then. For a half hour they tried to put a call through, but the lines were all jammed or else they received a busy signal. Losing patience, they finally called in their trusted Gestapo man to drive us to the train station.

It was the same fellow who had driven us to the soccer field! Only this time the white carnation had been replaced by a uniform!

As he drove he thanked us over and over again for not betraying him to his superiors. He offered to take us across the border, one by one, in the trunk of his car.

We couldn't trust him. How could we? No one had picked us up on the other side of the field so maybe it was a prearranged deal with the Gestapo. But, then again, he could have turned us in. Confusion led to a definite "thanks, but no thanks."

We arrived at the inn at Aachen. Marga and I went to bed, exhausted, with murmurings in the background about father making another attempt by himself that night.

At eight the next morning we came downstairs and found mother in tears.

"Children, you might as well forget it, because father left about four hours ago. Some really shady looking characters had come to pick him up and said he'd call in a half hour from Holland. He hasn't called.

"I have some pills. We might as well take them. There's no sense . . . for us to go on living . . . because father obviously is . . . is . . ."

"Mother!" Marga quickly broke her train of thought and insisted we wait just a while longer. She was seventeen, full of life and wasn't ready to abort an exciting future! I was always a very obedient child and would have taken the pill with no qualms whatsoever.

An hour later the phone call came. Father was so physically worn out his voice sounded strange to mother and she wasn't sure it was him. Yet, he spoke just the few Polish words they both knew. When speaking in front of Marga or me they would use Polish expressions meaning "she's the little one," or "time for them to go to bed."

"I don't know if it was really him," mother said as she hung up the phone.

Thirty minutes later he called again. His voice was more rested. The men who had taken him had lost their way, crisscrossing the country and at one point resting in a German guardhouse.

Father's heart was weak, a condition he said he obtained during a gas attack on the front lines while fighting for Germany in the first World War. He was a good German and even won a medallion.

It was difficult for him to keep up with the men as they dragged him through the swampland. A heavy coat weighed him down and finally the pressure of fatigue and anxiety gave way to hysteria.

He went blind. The men led him by the hand until they had reached their destination, a border town in Holland. They did this out of the "goodness of their hearts" instead of demanding money in advance.

Once safely rested in Holland father's sight returned and the first thing he saw was an open palm—waiting for payment before mother, Marga and myself would be taken across. We had promised the Gestapo we were returning to Berlin, so our first chance to leave was no longer available.

My father contacted the man running his business in Amsterdam and instructed him to send money, which he did. He found out later this man had been swindling him the entire time and didn't pick up our visas for us because he wasn't through fixing the books! This was the same as murder in those days. A visa would have meant an earlier release from prison for father.

Another car pulled up at the inn for us. Marga, always the brave one, shied away. She was reacting to three days of exposing raw nerves to a minute-by-minute drama and was now easily frightened.

After some gentle persuasion she steadied herself and climbed in. We headed for the border. Marga had a Dutch passport to use with the bearer's picture resembling a thirty-five-year-old matron. My mother's "picture" bore no resemblance to her either.

As for me, I had to pass for under eight. At just a couple months shy of sixteen, I was used to it.

What would happen at the border? I worried about being so "young," for didn't adults talk to children more than their parents? I didn't know a word of Dutch. We approached the border at night and curled up on the seat, each pretending to be asleep.

I thought they must be able to hear my heart pounding with such loudness. The guard's flashlight flickered from one passenger to another as he compared the passport photographs.

Either God blinded his eyes or someone had padded his wallet. He let us pass.

We met father in the village and boarded a train for Amsterdam. While on board I kept worrying about someone asking me a question in Dutch.

I spent several lifetimes in three days and for months and months the most horrendous nightmares would jar me loose from a heavy sleep.

Yet the experiences of fleeing Germany were gradually washed away under a growing flood of new persecution which was preparing to drown us in Amsterdam.

# CHAPTER SIX

# "Jood"

We had been in Amsterdam a short time when the Dutch arrested the men who had come across the border the way father had, to discourage others from entering Holland. He was taken to a refugee camp as one of many "examples." The men weren't treated badly, but camp is camp and mother was afraid father's heart would give out.

After a month she went to The Hague and discovered our visas had been ready for weeks, but no one had picked them up! With this the entire family legally emigrated from Germany and father was freed.

Soon after he came home Marga and I joined a Zionist youth group. As we attended our first meeting I heard a girl say, "Oh, for heaven's sake!"

It was Lore Zuckerberg, the tallest girl in the group, gazing for the first time at the shortest. In this case opposites (in height) were attracted and we became fast friends.

We spent many days going on outings to the country, playing "war games" which resembled hide-and-seek, or riding bicycles on leisurely tours of the city and open fields.

On Jewish holidays the youth group sold honey for the New Year or irises for Passover. The profits were sent to the Jewish National Fund to build Palestine and plant trees. I was immediately infected with a love for Palestine, dreams of a Jewish homeland and fulfillment of what Theodor Herzl, Austrian writer who founded Zionism, had written about.

I was in the hospital from October 1939 to March 1940. Exclusively for observation of my height problem. By this time my promise to God on the soccer field must have been slightly dimmed by my parents' insistence I be treated.

Marga and Lore kept me informed on the youth group's activities and I was thrilled to learn Isaiah had prophesied:

"For the LORD shall comfort Zion:
  he will comfort all her waste places;
  and he will make her wilderness like Eden,
  and her desert like the garden of the LORD;
  joy and gladness shall be found therein,
  thanksgiving, and the voice of melody."
                              (Isaiah 51:3)

Ezekiel, not to be outdone, mentioned the restoration of the land many times, and also wrote the great parable of the valley of dry bones in chapter 37 in which God promised to bring a scattered nation of Jews back to their homeland.

Hospital life wasn't miserable, but I would rather not have been there. I did learn to speak Dutch and helped nurses in a large ward, often going for walks with them during non-duty hours.

If the nurse instructed a patient not to eat breakfast it meant two things: one—you'd be hungry that morning and two—a test would be administered.

On my ward it either meant a tube down your throat for a stomach test or else a needle in your arm for a blood offering. Everyone preferred the blood test. Except me.

"I hope it's the stomach test! I hope it's the stomach!" The stares I received were not half as bad as what I went through to give a little of my life's fluid.

They could never find a vein to take my blood. This didn't stop them from trying, though. The arm. Nope. The hand. Not quite. The foot. Not likely.

The whole process was very painful and even now I'm very stingy with my blood. I have but one acceptable vein, and I study carefully any requests for its use!

After my release in March, 1940, I joined my father and a bookkeeper in exposing the man who had been swindling him and I took over as a very loyal employee.

Evenings were filled with business school where I learned to write letters in Dutch and also studied principles of bookkeeping. Father would dictate his correspondence in German and I translated into Dutch.

51

This was a time of great irritation when we heard about the White Paper which nullified the Balfour Declaration, thereby limiting emigration to Palestine. The youth group demonstrated against the White Paper. Peacefully.

*May 10, 1940.* I tossed restlessly in my sleep, hearing the sound of gunfire close by but passing the noise off as a bad dream.

It wasn't. Germany had attacked Holland. My family was awake at once and very excited. For the next five days we ran back and forth from an air raid shelter to our apartment. The shelter. Our apartment. The shelter. Our apartment. A constant race.

Each morning at five o'clock a city-wide alarm clock in the form of an ear-splitting siren shook us out of bed. I ducked back under the covers but Marga, tugging everyone towards the door, was anxious to get us all to the shelter.

One morning a sound which dwarfed the noise of the siren in intensity came directly at me and I instinctively hid beneath my blankets, praying the bomb would manage to skim the top of my head.

It exploded catercorner from our apartment. I found out later if you hear the bomb it has already passed, even though it sounds as if the opposite is true.

Dutch Jews began an exodus to the coast and took any boat they could find for safe passage to England. All Germans—us included—were not allowed on the street.

There were no hard feelings on our part, for the Germans were parachuting down and organizing their Fifth Column. They flattened Rotterdam, captured other cities and threatened to level Amsterdam.

The Dutch, fighting valiantly, surrendered after five days.

On the last day the curfew was lifted and we made a dash to the sea. All the boats were gone. Father, worried they would be coming for him, took a room in another apartment and went into hiding.

It was very scary. I never thought they would actually search for him, but mother said they did. Father stayed hidden for a year, seeing us as often as he thought it was safe.

Rotterdam was destroyed right after we were told to come finalize our visa applications for America. First the curfew kept us from going, then our papers were burned in the fire which swept the city.

Germany was in control, and each civilian had to register and be identified. We received a large "J" on our cards.

In 1941 mother became very ill. I believe she had TB but she disagrees. In any case, her lungs were never in top shape again. She said she went to a hospital for four weeks, but because of what the Germans were doing I must have completely wiped this from my memory.

With no warning the troops converged on a Jewish neighborhood and grabbed every youth from age seventeen to twenty-one they could find. Needless to say this was very upsetting and indicated what the conquerors had in mind for their victims.

The group was taken to Mauthausen. None returned.

Soon after this incident mother was taken to a rest home at Hilversum, twenty-seven kilometers from

Amsterdam. I stayed in a family hotel arrangement close by so that I could visit her during specific hours in the afternoons.

We had been there a few days when news arrived of a bomb falling just two blocks from where we lived. Two very short blocks! The information came by special delivery letter, so before I managed to open it my mind played a thousand tricks on me.

I expected terrible news about my family being hurt. Instead, the letter bawled me out—for taking the last butter stamp we had. Everything was rationed and butter was precious. They wanted me to mail the stamp back, but the bomb had upset me so that I jumped on my bicycle and rode about fifteen miles to home.

I arrived, panting heavily, and handed over the stamp to my family—my excuse for coming. They laughed about this for quite a while and I rushed all the way back in time to visit mother in the afternoon. She never knew a thing.

I was glad the bomb was from either Britain or America, yet it *was* in a residential neighborhood and I figured it might have . . .

*December 7, 1941.* We heard Japan had attacked Pearl Harbor. We danced for joy and hugged each other, happy that America had been forced into the war. We knew this would be a major factor in helping England to win.

Early in 1942 the Germans made us wear badges with the Star of David and "Jood" (Jew) written across it. As teenagers we didn't especially mind and even made jokes about it.

A well-known poem went something like:

"In the wonderful month of May, when all the roses spring up . . ." We changed it to:

"In the wonderful month of May, when all the roses bloom, then in my Jewish heart a little star came up." It rhymes in German.

We also said, "Wear the brown badge proudly, no Jew will die from it." Which, in a way, wasn't true. Our spirits were kept up nicely by our own morale boosters and by the friendliness of the Dutch people.

The gentile civilians of Amsterdam were wonderful, greeting us and giving us their seats on the streetcar or bus to show us the German monster of hate wasn't their idea. They went out of their way to prove they liked us and would help any way they could.

Dutch conductors went on strike in protest of another German roundup of Jewish children. They were forced to go back to work the next day—one of the disadvantages of being an occupied country. This signaled the end of public transportation for Jews.

Then they started sending German managers to Jewish-owned businesses. One would just walk in and say, "Here I am, I'm taking over."

After I was through with work one afternoon father called from his business and from the tone of his voice I knew.

"He's come?"

"Yes."

Mr. Schmidt was now boss. Comparatively speaking he wasn't as miserable a man as the others. But he did take all our money and control of the business.

It was my father's business, right? So after Schmidt takes over he fires me—because he can't employ too many Jews! He couldn't get along without father.

My feelings really weren't hurt, for I expected it.

Lore and I began to take lessons in making artificial flowers to be worn as corsages. With our profits from modest sales we took private lessons in English, literature and psychological testing. This last course evoked much laughter from my friends, but it did serve to occupy my mind.

In May of 1942 Marga became engaged to Eric Haas. Two months later we planned a birthday party for him on July 5, two days late. I rode up on my bicycle, the first guest to arrive, then left again to give them a little more time together. Very considerate. I wheeled around the block, leaned against the side of a church and waited for the others to show. When they came I followed them in. A very solemn atmosphere had replaced the hilarious kidding I expected from a birthday party.

During my quick ride a man had appeared with a summons for Eric. On the night of July 14 he was ordered to report at a railway station for transportation to a concentration camp.

# CHAPTER SEVEN

# Long Wait for Prison

I was dispatched posthaste to find my parents. Father usually could find a way to get people in these situations back on dry ground.

Within a few days Marga and I received similar summons. Thousands of Jewish youth our age had received orders to report July 14. Marga and Eric, with the erroneous notion families stay together in camp, decided to marry at once.

July 8, 1942, they were married in a civil ceremony. Four days later a rabbi came to our house and married them again—to make it *kosher*. The only ones laughing were the bride and groom, teasing each other about spitting into a common wine glass before passing it to the other.

July 13, the day before we were scheduled to leave, our doctor suggested I see a German physician and try to get off on medical grounds. I was nineteen. My hair was combed with a part down the middle and pulled over on each side as a little girl would wear it. Then cut short. Simply horrible.

Father took me to see the doctor. As we waited we saw Jewish men, women and children with a variety of illnesses being sent off to camp.

I was getting panicky. Marga and Eric were slated to travel to Auschwitz and I didn't particularly want to go. We hadn't heard what went on at Auschwitz, but it obviously wasn't good.

We never planned on how I would act with the doctor, yet somehow it came naturally from my previous experience of being a seven-year-old teenager in Germany. I pretended to be retarded.

"Where do you live?" the doctor asked.

"We live at . . . ." father started to answer, then . . . .

"I want *her* to answer!"

I mumbled very slowly.

"Do you ever go out on the street?"

"Yes . . . just to . . . the corner."

My courage was quite remarkable! I was scared stiff. Father interrupted the questioning and pleaded with them.

"Look at her little hands. Can't you leave her with us?"

Father addressed the man by the German equivalent of "Mr. Super Doctor," the title for a physician of high military rank. This was an important factor. The doctor, his ego well inflated, deferred me.

I believe at this point my name was scratched off the lists, for they never came looking just for me. I might have escaped by going into hiding but I chose to stay with the family. This same day Mr. Schmidt, our German manager, convinced the Gestapo that Eric and Marga were needed in the business. Father had just switched from ladies' wear to lining soldiers' coats with fur—a critical skill. Father employed as many Jews as he could to postpone their going to camp.

There were lists for everything, for those who worked for the German army to those helping the Jewish Agency sort out names. At first people tried to get on every list they could, hoping their jobs would keep them from camp. As time moved ahead the Germans, very nicely organized, used these same lists to pick up another trainload of forced labor for their camps or sick sacrifices for their ovens.

*August, 1942.* From our apartment we could hear a commotion. Through the window we could see the Germans had blocked off our street at either end and were methodically plucking Jewish tenants from their homes.

We watched them come from both sides. At last heavy boots pounded on the floor downstairs, only to scamper outside much quicker than they had entered! It seemed a woman, married to a man who had had a colostomy, had timed her daily routine perfectly. Just as the troops stormed in they found her cleaning the waste from her husband's sack and the smell drove them out! They never came upstairs.

Days later they forced Jewish families living in the suburbs to move in with families living in the city. A family moved in with us and they—like many others —turned out to be Christian Scientists, or "baptized

Jews." After exploring their beliefs I discovered they were neither Christians nor scientists.

Their name appeared on a list the Germans carried into our building one night. When the troops discovered several other Jews lived in the apartments they decided to have a field day and pick everyone up. This was perfectly "legal."

I was asleep in a small attic room, away from the others. I heard them march up the steps and a familiar lump once again lodged in my throat. My door was unlocked. There was usually no reason to lock it, but now . . . .

They confronted the father of the other children who also slept in the attic.

"Is anyone in the attic?" I was alone but he tried to protect me.

"No."

He wasn't too convincing and the soldier tried to open the door next to mine which led to a storage room. It was locked. Then he tried my door. I didn't breathe.

It clicked open. He fumbled for the switch, found it, and flooded the room with light. There I was.

"Get dressed!"

"As . . . soon as you leave I'll . . . get dressed," I stammered.

"No! Get dressed now!"

I had no choice. I climbed out from under the covers, tugged on my clothes, picked up a rucksack which was already packed and headed down the stairs.

"Go back!" other tenants warned me when they saw me coming.

"Forget it. They've already found me."

With a sorrowful expression I plodded into my parents' bedroom and found them both shaking badly. Keeping calm, they got up, put on their clothes and—bribed the guards.

We were three for five. Marga and Eric were taken away.

They herded my sister and brother-in-law into a crowd at a local Jewish theater, where people sprawled in the seats and in the aisles waiting to be transported to one camp or another. Most were taken from the theater to Westerbork, a camp in Holland. From there, most went to Auschwitz.

Marga and Eric were detained in the cramped theater for several days until Schmidt, once again, managed to have them released. They came home for a short while before the day arrived when we heard Goebbels on the radio declaring:

"We are going to destroy all the Jews, we will wipe them out!"

At that moment the doorbell rang.

Eric smiled. "That was prompt service!"

It wasn't a joke. I was taking a bath when I heard the heavy steps and bell. Right away I pulled on my camp clothes and grabbed my rucksack. The bell meant one thing, for it surely wasn't the milkman.

This particular list was for those working for the German army. Father, Marga and Eric. Mother and I weren't mentioned.

Back to the theater. After a couple of days good old Schmidt had my father released, but couldn't do anything for my sister and brother-in-law. Eric's uncle, owner of a bicycle shop, offered one of his vehicles, gifts and money to an official. The bribe worked. Marga and Eric were released after a week. The Jewish uncle had married a gentile so he was safe not only then, but during the entire war.

A few months later I was riding down a narrow side street on my way to pay Lore an afternoon visit. Suddenly a hand clamped down tight on my shoulder and I turned my head.

A strange man rode his bike next to me. The Dutch had been so nice to us that I didn't think twice when he attempted to hand me something. They often would give us vegetables, butter or eggs—things we couldn't buy. As I started to reach for it I realized what it was. My hand jerked back and I sped up. He was completely naked under his coat. At once his fingers darted all over my body, pinching me everywhere. He used language which, for the most part, I didn't understand.

We bicycled side by side. He didn't give an inch. He informed me with a sarcastic tone that this was what Jewish girls were for—to be used. He threatened to take me to the SS if I attempted to escape.

I started to throw up little "arrow" prayers to God —quick, urgent pleas for His help. My mind spun in a whirlpool of alternatives. Should I fall off the bike? Call to people on the street for help? (No, can't be sure I can trust them.) Keep on riding? What?

His hand retained a viselike hold on my shoulder. We came to a corner where I had to turn. I felt a renewed strength and my words burst through a shield of fear.

"I have to turn here!"

My bike shot to the left and he stayed with me. Once more, to the left, and he followed. I saw Lore's father's store in sight and raced for it. (Here her father ironed people's wash with a large round steam press.) I hopped off the bike, fumbled with the lock, and leaned heavily on the doorbell. He coolly sat on his bike. Watching. Waiting.

Lore's mother opened the door and I flew past her. My body heaved with deep sobbing for twenty minutes before she could draw out the story from me. After several minutes more the man left. One of my "arrows" had been answered. We couldn't call for help from anyone. The police would have believed whatever nonsense he told them over my version, for the Germans used to take Jews to the station for any reason imaginable.

Once a Jewish man was walking his dog when the animal did his business where he shouldn't have. The owner was taken by the police and impelled to perform a number of horrible things as punishment.

Soon the soldiers came to take inventory at our apartment. I glanced at them for only a moment. One of the troops resembled the man on the bike! I was too scared to make a positive identification, but for a second our eyes met in awkward recognition. I didn't dare say anything.

Lore was working for the Jewish Agency. Father offered to have her work for him, for we felt her chances of staying in the city were better. A great deal of debate was conducted between Lore and her parents before she came to us. She hated the work. Yet we couldn't delay the inevitable forever. Lore was taken away.

I left my bicycle locked up on Saturdays, the Sabbath, wanting to be a better Jew. My family thought this was ridiculous and I tried to do this without their knowing, but it never worked. I soon broke down under their laughter.

I gave up trying to keep the Sabbath, yet the desire to become right with God grew stronger. I received an Orthodox prayer book for my twentieth birthday, February 28, 1943.

Then—they came again. This time with all of our names on the list. We shoved our cat into our neighbor's care, picked up our rucksacks and walked to the corner to meet the truck.

Eric questioned my father. "Hey, what list are they picking up tonight?"

"The *frontkampfer*. The ones who fought on the front lines in the last war."

"Hey, I didn't fight in that war!" That was Eric.

"I put you on the list."

Two days of uncertainty passed in the theater before the magical Mr. Schmidt performed his duty for the business and got us out under the "five Schlamms." This almost didn't work since Eric and Marga's last name was Haas.

I returned home with stiff joints and an army of fleas in my blanket. The tiny pests loved me very much. It must have been my sweet blood.

Upon our return the neighbor informed us our cat, called either *Jantje* or *Pietje*—two good Dutch names—wouldn't stay with her and had been waiting by our door. Very unusual for a cat.

We kept hearing a "meow, meow," but couldn't determine where it was coming from. We weren't allowed on the streets after the eight o'clock curfew. We opened the closets. The cupboards. Looked under the beds. Finally he was spotted in the downstairs garden. We couldn't go out into the street in order to get to the garden so we yelled to a gentile neighbor to bring the cat up for us. The poor thing was sick. Marga brought it to a veterinarian the next day and received the diagnosis—homesickness.

He missed us! That night he made the rounds of each lap, purred softly, then crawled off and died while we said *kiddush* to usher in the Sabbath. He was killed by unbearable sadness.

*June 20, 1943.* The streets were blocked off before the Germans drove through with loudspeakers ordering all Jews to prepare for camp. We shoveled leftovers into our stomachs, got our things together and waited.

They came after us for the fourth time. The camps which the Dutch had started for refugees were taken over by the victors and we didn't know a great deal about them. A brief stay in the theater preceded a ride in a freight car to Westerbork.

We jumped down from the train and marched into camp. Barracks were assigned to each person, but I came out ahead of the others. My doctor in Amsterdam had asked a Jewish colleague at camp to take care of me. I stayed in the hospital—a great privilege. Mother and Marga stayed in a woman's barrack while father and Eric stayed with the men. Friends of ours, who had lived there as illegal immigrants before the Germans took over, had a little apartment.

Regardless of where you slept the same thing happened at three o'clock every Tuesday morning. The lights went on. A voice boomed. The names of one thousand Jewish prisoners were read for a transport to Auschwitz.

This was the horrible part about Westerbork. You never knew who would be called. Compared to other camps, Westerbork was paradise, but the Tuesday morning ordeal was terribly nerve-wracking.

We had everyday chores, but not forced labor like later on. Jews responsible to the Germans led us in a self-government type of situation. We constantly looked for things to do to occupy the endless hours.

Within a few days father was released to return to his work. It was a difficult decision for him to make. He had no guarantee the rest of us wouldn't disappear on the next transport.

"Look," mother told him, "whether you're here or not we might go to Auschwitz. You can't prevent it. We'd rather take the chance of your leaving with the possibility you can get us out too."

There were only five companies doing the work of lining coats with fur, so father was a special craftsman. He sadly returned to our apartment to find the place completely ransacked. The furniture was gone, pictures ripped to shreds and all valuables missing. A common practice. As soon as a Jewish family was led away the German troops took what they could. An open door invited former neighbors to finish the job.

I prayed to God that somehow He'd release us again. After two weeks of a monotonous existence at Westerbork father managed to get mother and me out. I'm really not sure how. We lost the excitement of being free in the midst of a naked apartment. We found another place for a month until ours was repaired, then moved back in. Marga and Eric, who had lived with us since their marriage because apartments were scarce, were still at Westerbork, so had no need for their room.

We made this a "packing" room. If we came across some canned groceries we'd store them there. We'd also bake solid pound cakes, with real eggs and butter our gentile friends scraped together for us on the black market. We sent the cakes and homemade bread to our friends at various camps. We knew from firsthand experience the necessity of receiving food. Often the cake or bread would contain money. I did this for Lore, but the guards caught on to this trick and would slice up all of the incoming treats. You either stopped sending money or took a chance an inspector's knife would miss the enclosure.

A person receiving a package at camp had to sign a printed card. It was the custom for a woman to sign both her maiden and married name before the card was returned to the sender. Lore, a single girl, would write "great" or "wonderful" for her married name to show her appreciation.

Lore's cousin in Sweden, whom I had never met, wanted to send her a package. I told him to send it to me and I would forward it. I was afraid he'd give her sweets which she didn't need. He didn't know me, yet reluctantly granted my wish. I took the things he had sent and wrapped them again in his paper turned inside out.

Previously the cards had come back marked Lore Zuckerberg Great or Lore Zuckerberg Wonderful. This time it was signed Lore Zuckerberg Magnus—

her cousin's last name—to acknowledge the sender's name scribbled originally in Sweden.

We met a man who had been at Vught, another camp, but was released because his wife was a gentile. He reported that no one was allowed to do anything at Vught, and that this made it impossible to hang on to one's sanity.

*July 12, 1943.* Marga and Eric were sent to Vught. We had been home about a week. Marga smuggled in an iron to take the wrinkles from both her clothes and morale. This was a definite spirit booster. Like taking a nap when you were supposed to work or talking when you shouldn't. Little things.

Through his firm father could employ a group of workers at Vught to do his fur-lining work. Various firms would pay the Germans so much per piece for what was done by camp laborers. The Germans at camp had a quota of so much money to earn each day rather than quantity of goods: the more father paid the helpers the easier it was on them.

A Jewish messenger would deliver work to be done to the camp and bring back the finished goods. He was a good friend of Marga's. In his attaché case, among other things, would go a sandwich or quarter of a chicken for Marga and Eric. He'd leave the case in a deserted room. My sister would sneak in, "steal" the food meant for her and quietly leave. She also left messages to be returned to us.

Vught was far worse than Westerbork. A real concentration camp. Eric was forced to roll in the thick mud over and over for either the guards' amusement or for punishment. The food was atrocious.

The eve of Rosh Hashanah (the Jewish New Year)

was almost upon us when father came home and said, "Tonight they're going to pick us up." This was September 28, 1943. We had had three more months of liberty. We stayed up very late packing all the food we could. The morning sun woke us—and nothing had happened.

The next day we prepared to welcome in the New Year when father came home with the same message, "Tonight for sure." He knew it was time for the five men running the fur shops to be taken. They had all agreed beforehand not to go into hiding and jeopardize the others, but at this point two did anyway. It really didn't matter.

Having prepared the night before, we went to sleep fairly early. I woke at six o'clock—precisely when the doorbell rang. I thought it was nice to have slept through the night.

We opened the door and admitted our expected visitors. The long wait was finally over and I sighed with relief. For the fifth time we marched in rhythm to the sound of combat boots at our heels.

This time we didn't get off.

# CHAPTER EIGHT

# Gam Zeletauvo

The shock of the unknown was missing, since we had been at Westerbork before, but the uncertain status of a permanent camp resident crept over us.

During the last few days of our freedom, we had sent food packages in to our friends. So when we were taken to Westerbork, we enjoyed some of our own delicious cake. Within a few days after our arrival, another friend gave us a loaf of bread we had shipped to him earlier.

Mother and I shared a bunk, covered by a luxurious down-filled quilt we had brought. During the night we were sprinkled by a young child sleeping above us. Amused, we wondered if this could be a good omen.

I stopped by the hospital to say hello to the doctor who had been so nice to me during my first visit. Remembering I was enthusiastic about working with children, he offered to let me stay in a barrack which had been converted to a make-shift maternity ward.

Marga wasn't with us this time in Westerbork, so I felt it was up to me to watch out for mother. She was feeling poorly and her eyesight was not good. Reluctantly I said no to the doctor's offer.

"Think about it. You can still decide."

I forced the option from my mind and plodded back to the barrack where father had some startling news for me. He and mother were being sent to Vught.

Previously they had wanted me to go into hiding. My small size and gentile looks were a definite asset. Yet, as they told me of their transfer, they didn't insist I try to come along. I was under twenty-one. Perhaps I could have joined them if I had desired.

I hadn't gone into hiding but had demanded that I stay with my family so I could always know where they were. Now when I thought of going with them to Vught, a burdensome uneasiness urged me to decline a chance to go with them. We all agreed.

I watched them climb onto a truck, carrying a few possessions, realizing it might be the last time we would see each other. Within a few days after returning to Westerbork I had been left alone with my thoughts.

Marga, when she heard my parents were coming to Vught, put everything in motion for me to join them just as I had been setting up roadblocks to prevent my transfer.

Lore, also at Vught, wrote to say it had been the greatest disappointment of her life when I didn't hop off the truck with my parents. She had already reserved a good bunk for me. I doubted this would be the biggest disappointment of her life, but I appreciated the thought.

Father had said they would try to return to Westerbork on the next transport back from Vught. Childishly, I believed him. I thought they had a choice, but I should have known they could only try —and very few were successful.

I prayed they'd come back soon. My fellow Jewish prisoners comforted me and previous ties with the Zionist youth group flaired to a peak of loyalty as the harassment increased.

When you're persecuted you can't help but feel a family kind of love for the others being tormented around you. I believe God has used the constant persecutions since Abraham to help knit the Jewish people together and permanently weld their nation into the twisted sculpture of history. We, as a nation, have always seemed to benefit from the grace of God in escaping total annihilation.

On Yom Kippur, the Day of Atonement when each good Jew confesses his yearly sins before God and asks for forgiveness, I got a strange idea into my head. My parents, I felt, would be back in time for Chanukah (Festival of Lights). This became my deadline for them to return to Westerbork. About three months away.

The dust from the truck carting my parents away had barely settled before I had eagerly accepted the doctor's offer. I found myself, a tiny young woman, lost in a ward full of pregnant women and crying babies.

Then—a woman in the ward contracted polio. This was before vaccines had been invented, and they did the only thing possible. They quarantined us for six weeks.

What a blow. Our friends with the small apartment had offered to be my "parents" now that I was separated from mine, but here I was shut into the barrack with the others. A fence was hastily erected around our area—skipped a few feet—then put up another barrier. Visitors stood outside of the far fence and shouted to us.

A transport arrived from Vught. One of the travelers clung to the fence and advised me my parents were in good shape. In Vught. Why hadn't they come? I couldn't figure it out at first, then realized they had no choice.

The month and a half of being held in a prison within a prison passed slowly.

One of the items our family brought with us was a special comb to run through our hair and check for lice. I had that comb with me. Right after the quarantine was lifted I was sitting on my bed, playing with the comb, when I asked a friend, "How do you know when you have a louse? I've never had one."

"When you have one," she laughed, "you'll know it!"

The next second I looked at the comb and saw something crawling on it. Kind of like an animated speck of dandruff, only bigger, and a sickening gray-green color. I didn't say another word. I knew.

The man in charge of the "lice inspection" was the

same one who headed the Christian Science family who had stayed with us. If someone had lice it meant just one thing: a shaved head.

The miserable hygienic conditions in camp were ideal for the breeding of lice. Nothing we could do about it. The man's wife did me a tremendous favor and supplied me with special shampoo to wash my head. I carried the shampoo with me to my barrack, ran the comb through my hair and found three more of the ugly creatures. I was becoming scared. I hurried to my friend's apartment, a nicer place to wash, but she wouldn't let me in! They, too, were afraid of lice.

At night, in my own barrack, I tried nonchalantly to scrub my head—hoping no one would notice and assume I had lice. Very embarrassing. The next morning the woman took me to the lice inspection barrack.

"She thinks she may have lice, will you check her?"

We never mentioned I had already been attacked by the things, for this would have meant an instant shave job. I passed the test, narrowly missing a smooth scalp.

*Gam zeletauvo,* I thought, *everything works for the good.* For during the rest of camp this same tube of shampoo kept the lice away.

Rumors circulated about a transport coming from Vught to Westerbork. I expected my parents to be on it. Then we discovered the transport was simply going to stop outside of Westerbork, wait for some of our people to board, then head straight for Auschwitz. I toyed with the idea of volunteering for Auschwitz. I couldn't let my parents go without me. Several friends talked me out of this, convincing me I had no assurance my parents would be on the train.

A friend managed to transfer my name from the Palestine list to the South American list, since all those listed under Palestine were slated for this transport to Auschwitz.

The next day the doctor said he had crossed me off the list. It was his prerogative to prevent any person from traveling if he wasn't in good health. This was rather ironic, since the Germans gassed you at the end of the line anyway. They merely wanted their one thousand a week from Westerbork. Numbers were all important—not souls.

I found out later I would have been taken if he hadn't crossed me off the list; and if I had been at Vught I wouldn't have been spared. My father was slapped in the face several times before successfully keeping them from taking mother.

Anyone who wasn't able to perform hard labor or participate in a critical skill, such as lining coats with fur or assembling parts for Phillips radio, was being sent off to Auschwitz and a speedy death. Phillips did a lot for the Jewish people by allowing them to take as much work as possible and thereby delay an even more tragic fate.

The November 15 transport passed us by, carrying hundreds of glassy-eyed Jews with no food, no clothing and no tomorrow.

In December a little baby was delivered to our barrack. Charltje—little Charles—an uncircumcised ten-month-old child who had been discovered in his hiding place in the city. Before coming to Westerbork he had spent one week in jail, where others must have taken care of him. Somehow the Germans had decided he was Jewish. Charltje was obviously in no position to defend himself!

I was responsible for being his adopted mother, complete with feeding, washing, changing diapers and gently pinching his cheeks. It was impossible. Impossible to take care of that baby and not fall hopelessly in love with him!

As it drew close to Chanukah my dream of seeing father and mother grew stronger against a tide of friendly skepticism.

People in camp tried everything to get a postponement from leaving Westerbork and going to the extermination centers. One way to do this was to have a visa for Palestine. We had that. Another method was to obtain a passport from Ecuador or Uruguay through embassies in Sweden or Switzerland.

Eric's uncle, the one with the bike shop, had an employee whose father-in-law lived in Sweden. The daughter and son-in-law received Swedish citizenship papers through her father while they were in hiding from the Gestapo. They had a difficult decision to make. Take a chance, come out of hiding and hope they'd be allowed to go to Sweden, or else place themselves at the whim of the Gestapo. They risked it. They left the secrecy of their room and confronted the Germans—who let them go to Sweden.

Once there they found Eric's cousin, who explained that the South American passports our family had were given out by the embassies, but not recognized as being legal by the countries themselves. They were all fakes. I believe these relatives and friends in Sweden were responsible for our passports later being legalized for the duration of the war.

A German woman, compiling a correct list, came to Westerbork to take care of those Jews with these passports. Those with papers for Palestine or South America were being sent to a special concentration camp at Bergen-Belsen. Special because it didn't have gas chambers like the others.

It fell on me to convince this woman of the necessity of my parents returning from Vught to Westerbork since the family was listed on one passport. The idea germinated in my mind for weeks and brought me a little bit closer to a state of frightened panic as the day drew closer for me to see her.

She was due to arrive on Monday. She didn't come, but they promised she would show on Thursday. She didn't. Try next Monday. No woman. Thursday. Not this time. This went on and on with my fears soaring up one emotional ski jump after another before landing in a soft slush of disappointment.

One Friday morning—and Friday was my lucky day—a woman in my barracks was called out to see this person. She had finally arrived! My first reaction was quite normal. I ran for the bathroom.

It was my turn. As I cautiously made my way toward her door a friend encouraged me.

"The 'no' you have in your pocket already. She can always say 'no,' but maybe she'll say 'yes.'"

With a machine-gun delivery I told her my parents were in Vught and I was in Westerbork and we were all listed on the same passport and please couldn't she do something so we could all get together? Whew.

"They are? Give me their names and birthdates."

I rattled these off, then speedily mentioned Marga and Eric were on the same passport. More names and birthdates. Fortunately I remembered Eric's.

On the way out of the office I casually asked her what she thought the chances were of their coming to Westerbork.

"It looks encouraging," she said, "but we're very busy."

This was December 17, 1943, the Friday before Chanukah which began the next Tuesday. I figured if the Maccabees could burn oil for eight days with a one-day supply then God could bring my family back. Somehow.

I happily went to some friends and told them I had talked to the woman and everything would be fine. It's almost Chanukah! They had to calm me down with several injections of camp reality.

Monday I received a message that my parents would be transported from Vught to Westerbork, but grammatically the verb was in the future future sense—very distant. The office said they would be on the next transport although none were planned. How could this be? The next day was Chanukah! I gave myself a week's leeway. After all, Chanukah *did* last eight days.

I checked my food supply. I had eight eggs ready. For weeks I put the new egg on the bottom of my cache and ate the old one on top. Eight was the most I could keep without them rotting. People thought I was crazy, but I expected to have a big family reunion.

That afternoon I asked another man about the

transport. He got a twinkle in his eye, winked, and said it would be pretty soon. I couldn't tell if this was fact or encouragement.

Monday night I entreated the doctor to admit my mother to the hospital when she arrived. He said he couldn't admit her before she had come. If she did come, and was really sick, he'd do his best. He went off on a tangent, warning me not to be so optimistic in the face of such poor odds and uncertain events.

His words of wisdom didn't make a dent in my faith. Then, before I could dismiss myself from this unnecessary advice, a messenger interrupted our conversation to suggest I come to another barrack at once.

Father, mother, Marga and Eric had just arrived!

# CHAPTER NINE

# Bergen-Belsen
# Wedding Anniversary Trip

This must be unique in the history of Nazi concentration camps. My family was the only one transported from Vught solely to bring them to Westerbork. No others. The Germans gave no reason for the action, but for me it was simply a direct answer to prayer.

Father and Eric had shorn heads, a trademark of the men at Vught. We dipped into my cache at our first opportunity and in one day they devoured the results of weeks of storing—stuffing the unexpected food into their mouths as children would do at a birthday party.

Between mouthfuls Charltje's proud "grandparents" eyed him affectionately and within two or three minutes had established a deep love for the baby. I tried desperately to legally adopt him. It couldn't be done.

He had been with me about a month, just long enough to become firmly attached to him, when one Tuesday morning at three o'clock his name was called. Charltje, just learning to stand, snuggled up to me.

I was given a basket from a friend and frantically went from bed to bed literally begging for diapers and things to send with him. I pinned a note on the basket to explain what foods he was eating.

My slight hopes of his continued existence were shattered when a burly guard came for Charltje, yanked him from me and swung the baby by his feet toward the train. Charltje went straight to Auschwitz and, in all probability, to the gas chamber. An eleven-month-old child couldn't do much work for the Führer.

For as long as I was at Westerbork I burst into tears as I passed his bunk. He was like my own.

*February 16, 1944.* My parents' twenty-fifth wedding anniversary. For years and years mother said she wasn't going to be home on this date, but would be traveling in celebration of the event. She got her wish.

They put us on a train for Bergen-Belsen.

To celebrate their anniversary we dug into a number of tiny spreads, like dips, we had made from a variety of food. We were quite proficient at it.

We sat in the last compartment on a typical European train, eating and laughing away the hours. I told them I believed we would all make it through the war. I didn't believe in being blown about by bad news or good news, feeling either depressed or happily expectant of release. I asked them if they thought the Allies would win or not. If they believed it then they shouldn't become depressed when hit with bad news. Just believe.

During the trip we were entertained by warped wood and Eric's sense of humor. Our compartment was right next to the bathroom. Each time a person using the facilities wished to leave, the door jammed and Eric heroically jumped to his feet to tug it open.

"Allow me," he smiled. The person usually turned several shades of red and hurried off.

When we arrived at Bergen-Belsen the laughing stopped.

We had ridden all night, stopping a few miles outside of the main camp by the next morning. As the train squeaked to a halt we were greeted by a welcoming committee composed of grumbling guards and growling German shepherd dogs. They resembled each other.

"Get out, you Jordan splashers!" they screamed. Jordan splashers? This was a new term for us, and seemed very funny. We knew what they meant.

They couldn't have been more harsh or cruel. We lined up, carrying our leftover food, clothes in a big box and lice in the clothes. We marched several miles to camp. On the way people would see us tramping along and would jeer at us, saying, "Hah! Some more Jews are coming!"

Ice and snow carpeted the ground. We reached our

destination and stood still. For the entire day we stood and stood and stood, the numbing cold biting into our limbs. We took turns supporting mother, who could barely stand.

At last we were assigned to a barrack and the race was on. Everyone scrambled to find a good bunk. My tiny legs kept me a few paces back from the others but I managed to grab a good home. The bunk, that is. *Home.* Where you kept everything you owned.

The next day mother started spitting blood so they took her into the main compound's hospital. Visitors were not permitted and we lost contact with her. We managed to find someone we could trust in her compound to take soup from us over the fence and bring it to her.

The ways of camp life became quickly evident as a man we knew traded a pair of shoes for some food—thereby setting a precedent for us. As long as we had a stitch of clothing left which we felt we didn't need we would trade it for food, usually with the Greek Jews in another barrack. For some reason the Greek Jews were rather privileged, and a Greek was in charge of the camp as far as our people were concerned. Although he was under German command, he did have some power and could obtain better food for his barrack.

At the time we arrived they were low on clothes and we had no food. We swapped.

*February 28, 1944.* My twenty-first birthday. Father and Marga urged me to beg this camp elder for permission to see my mother since it was a special day. I don't know why they insisted, for I didn't think he would care one hoot if it was my birthday. He didn't.

People would walk around the compound, straining their eyes to see conditions in other parts of the complex and make mental notes where they didn't want to go. From the little contact we had with the main camp we knew it wasn't a picnic.

They discussed how they could avoid winding up in a worse situation. How stupid, I thought. Who are we to decide?

The major strain of camp life was generated by daily harassments, not the sadistic measures most commonly publicized about concentration camps. Midnight showers are an example, forcing us to shiver in the cold of night instead of enjoying warmer temperatures in the day.

Often they'd herd us together for a sudden head count. You never knew what might happen next. Glimpses of neighboring camp areas, old rumors and new threats blended into a moment-by-moment abstract of barbarous art.

After a couple of weeks we were moved into a main part of camp, one of forty different areas at Bergen-Belsen. On one side of us were Hungarian Jews and, on the other, one of the worst spots in the compound. Anne Frank had been in that area, and although I didn't know her I spoke with several persons who did. She wasn't famous then—her diary wasn't discovered until later—but I knew of her and which transport she was in.

We violated orders when secretly communicating with people in this adjacent camp. They had no barracks during the icy winter months, just tents.

Scarcely any clothes. We watched them walk around with blankets tugged tightly around their slender bodies. Some didn't have blankets.

They were treated with more severity than most. One day the Germans snatched all their children from them and took them away. They could only stare as part of themselves disappeared forever. We knew at any time it could happen to us.

At our new location I was assigned to the Greeks' barrack, a very lucky break. Marga was placed in an ordinary barrack and couldn't join me. Yet I could "lower" myself and voluntarily switch positions with someone in Marga's group. I did.

During this time I read a book which dealt with a minister or priest (no difference to me), who was a real *goniff,* a real crook. This book taught me for the first time that persons in positions of religious leadership aren't necessarily deserving of man's worship or respect. I had considered clergymen to be saints on earth, standing majestically on a golden pedestal. Then I was alarmed to discover even our rabbis weren't all *kosher.*

Rabbis were in charge of several barracks. Soon they fell victim to the rarefied air a high position of authority gives and they joined other elders in discriminating against their own people.

Large vats of thin, watery soup constituted our meal each day. Maybe a turnip would be floating conspicuously on top. *Maybe.* Or a small piece of horsemeat or chunks of potato resting on the bottom. These were occasions to celebrate, for this type of food made infrequent appearances.

The barrack leaders learned how to flick their wrist

when serving the soup so heavy pieces of food would slip from the ladle back into the pot. After we had been given the watery soup they dug into what was left—the thick stuff on the bottom. Rules dictated they give seconds if any remained—beginning alphabetically—but after the elders had eaten two or three helpings for themselves there was usually nothing left.

In addition to the one liter of soup we received, we also were given a four-centimeter square of bread, roughly one and a half inches. Rarely we obtained a pat of margarine, restaurant-size, or else a triangle of rotting cheese.

There were days when we received nothing at all. Still others when we were handed a cup of water with dried parsley sprinkled lightly on top.

During our first month at Bergen-Belsen father's job was to rip up piles of old shoes taken from those less fortunate than us. He had to cut them at the seams, a difficult task, and was not allowed to cut into the leather. If he slipped a guard would slap his face.

He was fifty-four. You had to be fifty-five or sixty to get into the older people's barrack. That's an advantage we had at Bergen-Belsen. There was a barrack for old people and one for the sick. At Auschwitz the old and sick went directly to the gas chambers.

A doctor transferred father to the old people's barrack. Each day I would visit him he would perk up and ask, "Is the food coming yet? Is it thick or thin today?"

As soon as the food had left the kitchen it brought

with it rumors of its consistency. Thick or thin. This was extremely important and often had sole possession of your thoughts. Thick or thin. Thick or thin.

Food had such a firm grasp on your life, literally spelling the difference between the bunk and the grave, that some women began a strange practice. They exchanged recipes. I couldn't stand to watch the women write down all the wonderful things you could make with imaginary ingredients, mixed in a dream-world kitchen and eaten in a swirling universe of fantasy.

The recipes were real, but from the past. For the older women it helped satisfy their longing for food. It brought me no relief at all.

After the war we found a recipe mother had written for chocolate pudding. It said use one egg per person, then proceeded to list other ingredients and cooking instructions. At the very end was a brief note: If only for the family use just one egg for the entire batch. Humph! We thought the family should come first.

Women with children under three years were given milk. Most exchanged their ration for food rather than give it to the child. I took advantage of this, exchanging a full cup of soup for a half cup of milk. One day I'd bring the milk to my father. Then mother got her turn the following afternoon. I ate hardly anything.

I divided my inch-and-a-half square of bread into three parts. One third I gave to Eric, who burned up a lot of energy while working as a garage mechanic, one third went to father and one third for me.

I cut off the crust, saved it, then began to play my

favorite game of seeing how many slices I could cut from the remaining piece. The more pieces, the greater the satisfaction. I averaged six slices, which I ate at night, feeling like a real pig after the sixth slice slid down my throat. I really was gorging myself! The next morning I would slowly chew on the crust I had cut off.

Once in a while Marga would ask if I would lend her a quarter-ration or perhaps a third-ration. Everything had definite values, with margarine worth a quarter-ration of bread and cheese demanding a third-ration. I'd give the requested ration to Marga, realizing she could never catch up in order to pay me back. It took a tremendous effort on my part to hand over a pat of margarine, which to me was the same as ice cream. I teased it, sucked on it, let it linger on my tongue and very gradually felt it flow between my lips. It was so sweet.

This infrequent indulgence brought a tremendous sense of guilt to me, but the temptation was too strong to resist. Margarine, worth less than cheese on the camp's unwritten priority code, was more precious to me than cheese.

"Marga," I cried out one night, "would you like to exchange your margarine for my cheese?"

Her voice was immediately drowned out by several eavesdroppers who were quite willing to make the switch for the better profit. Our slight diet had its permanent effect on me. My legs are still swollen from hunger edema suffered in camp.

Holding my cup of milk very carefully one day, I stepped out from the barrack and ran right into a man in a hurry. He inadvertently knocked me into a small ditch. The milk was gone. A man going from millionaire to pauper because of a crash on the stock market was in no more tragic a situation.

The man who bumped into me was from the Greek barrack. The next day, so it wouldn't be a total loss, he made up for the incident by giving me an extra portion of soup. Milk was a treasured item. Some days the temptation to take a tiny sip overpowered me and I succumbed, only to discover it was even harder after a taste to resist it.

Eric and Marga were now the only ones from our family to have jobs. Eric in the garage and Marga sorting clothes taken from prisoners at Auschwitz. Clothes no longer needed. I didn't find this out until recently, for at the time she said she mended socks for the guards—which she did in part. Marga couldn't bear to tell us about sorting the clothes. Clothes from those who had been gassed. Different clothes she recognized. Clothes from close friends.

Occasionally the German man Eric or Marga worked under would give them an errand to run to the kitchen. This was a tremendous privilege, for the cooks were fairly nice and would allow messengers to eat as much bread, margarine and jam as they wanted. Yet when you're starved there's an absolute limit to what you can physically force down your throat into your stomach. They'd eat as much as possible, then give their regular ration to my parents.

Our family, the five of us, always shared everything and worked as a harmonious unit. It went without saying. Eric would share pickles with us he had snatched or mother would hand Eric a piece of bread through the window on his way to work.

Most families fought. Husband and wife. Parents and children. Arguing over a tiny piece of bread or snip of cheese. Constant bickering and verbal battles.

After the war many parents broke down and cried, confessing how they had taken a few spoonfuls of soup for themselves while carrying it to a sick child. Starvation accentuated an already selfish nature in man.

The ritual of passing out bread took extreme concentration. Some loaves were crumbly in the middle. Crumbly bread gave you nothing bread.

The person handing out bread liked me, waving me out of line when she had a poor loaf. She'd give it to a family she didn't like. I normally would have insisted on my regular turn, wishing to be fair. Since Eric's and now Marga's portions are involved, too, I accepted this favor.

After the war one of the bread distributors, a Jewish woman, wanted me to vouch for her and tell how nice she had been. I couldn't do it. Her kindness toward me didn't erase the fact she was quite horrible to others.

Our main area gate was left open since many of our people worked in other parts of Bergen-Belsen. A youth once spotted a heap of rotting turnips outside of the gate and rushed across to get some. As punishment the entire camp didn't eat the next day, which was *Tishah-b'Ab*—the day when the great Jewish temple in Jerusalem was destroyed. It was traditionally a day of fasting, so with great joy we accepted our penalty although it was difficult.

The Germans would sporadically give us bread for an entire week, a treacherous thing when you're half-starved. This amounted to a one or two-day supply of bread in normal living. I believe this was calculated since few could successfully ration it for themselves.

We had been sleeping one to a bunk, but the day came when a new variety came with built-in lice at no extra cost to us. Two in a bunk. Two-feet wide with wooden slats on the side to prevent even a cramped stretch of the limbs. These bunks were stacked three high, instead of the old two, and squeezed together with a narrow twelve to eighteen-inch passageway in between. In a two-bunk setup twelve people could scratch each other's back.

All food and clothes were kept in that half-bed under the mattress or in a tiny box at the foot. We practically had to tie our clothes down since the lice were almost walking off with our things, scampering up and down everywhere.

I hate to admit it but—I hardly ever washed. The bathroom, located between two barracks, was shared by both men and women. Cleanliness subdued modesty for many and men and women stripped and washed in front of each other. I couldn't. It was too cold.

Summers at camp have been fogged in my memory by the more dramatic weather of winter which kept me shivering constantly. Mother had made me some wrist warmers which nearly covered my fingers. I'd wash the tips of my fingers and splash water on my face.

Showers were infrequent. I hated them. I always felt dirtier afterwards than before I entered. They would shove the entire barrack, perhaps four hundred people, into a small anteroom where a smirking German guard stared at us as we got undressed. Clothes were put on a hanger before we stepped through a delousing process.

Naked women—emaciated, sick, covered with skin diseases, trembling from illness or the cold—were pushed into shower rooms. Four women for each outlet, touching, squirming and trying to get a little wet from a pencil-thin stream of water.

They put us through this about once a month. When I expected a sprinkling I'd sneak out to mother's barrack and hide under her blanket for a couple of hours. The danger of being caught was worth the reprieve, but I couldn't make it every time.

Marga had heard stories about camps worse than ours, and what went on at their "showers". When they woke us in the middle of the night for our first early morning shower Marga wouldn't let me go. She was sure we would be gassed.

Each person over the age of sixteen had to work. When they dismissed those under that every day I fell in line and marched back to the barrack. This was agreed to by the Greek *macher* (elder). Once a guard ran after me, ordered me to halt and asked how old I was. A quick decision was necessary. Tell him I was under sixteen and chance it, or tell him the truth? I stuck with the truth. He didn't say anything when I told him I was twenty-one. The German had wanted to see if I would lie. As he walked away I felt myself laboriously putting back together my scared, splintered psyche.

The enormity of Bergen-Belsen ruled out any opportunity for escape. We were kept in just one of many compounds. To get to the actual camp exit took several miles of walking or running past endless barbed wire, guards and bright lights all night long. Attempted escape meant successful suicide.

After the morning roll call the workers went to their jobs and the children hiked back to the barracks to be counted. And counted. And counted. The correct figure never materialized. Someone wouldn't return in time from the bathroom, another was sick in his bunk or perhaps they forgot to count the recent deaths.

The elder would attempt to arrive at the number the guards wanted. Often, just as he arrived at the right number, someone would walk up and he'd whisper hoarsely:

"Go away! It's just working out! Don't mess it up!"

This took at least an hour or two. Then a guard might spot a three-year-old squatting, the minimum age for those who had to stand, and he'd make us stay in formation another hour or two.

There were days and days when we stood in heavy rain or driving snow from early morning until evening when the others returned from a hard day's work and grudgingly joined our ranks.

If we were lucky enough to be detained only an hour or two I raced the others to the barrack and stood in line for three portions of soup—for me, Marga and Eric. When they came from a work-break to eat they could sit, gulp it down and return to work within a five-minute time limit.

My sister and brother-in-law enjoyed eating alone together in the summer. I ran back and forth trying to get three low, four-legged stools together for them. Two for chairs and one for a table. I could only carry two at a time. I'd dash to the spot, put down the stools, run back for two more and sprint once again to the eating place and discover at least one stool missing. Back again and again. Maybe five or six times until I had three saved.

Being at home each day also allowed me to do the wash for the family, a great time-saver for them and hard work for me.

Marga was a tremendous builder of our morale, constantly trying to make things as nice as possible. She even made a little tablecloth to fit over a bread box. For as long as we were at Bergen-Belsen she would say, "The war will be over in two months!"

Her reputation for optimism spread through the camp. As soon as she left from visiting father the other men would ask what she told him, as if she knew more than the others. Their hope was founded upon Marga's words, even though she very seldom heard any news where she worked.

Books were scarce. A book was passed around until all had read it before it was used for more practical purposes in the bathroom. A necessary fact of life! The only book I read was Charles Dickens' *A Christmas Carol*, which seemed to be a strange volume to be floating around Bergen-Belsen.

As a teenager I had read *Ben Hur*, only to be amazed later on to find that it was a Christian book —I didn't remember that part at all. I just knew a Jewish boy dropped an object from a roof accidentally and was sent to the galleys. The injustice of it stayed with me.

In August of 1944 a transport left for Palestine with a large number of people having the right papers. A token gesture from the Germans to maintain a rather transparent front for the outside world. About two hundred left, including a school friend of mother's.

Later we began receiving packages through the Red Cross from American relatives. We asked for hand cream and anything with fat, like butter. Jewish people like fat . . . .

A package arrived for us containing a jar full of some kind of substance which resembled either hand cream or fat—we couldn't tell. Only one way to find out. We dipped a finger into whatever it was and gingerly tasted it. We still couldn't tell. With hand cream or fat before us we opted for the fat and spread it on bread. Its true identity was never discovered.

"If a package comes for me," Marga would say, "don't wait until I come home from work, but divide it into five parts right away!" Our family shared everything with no second thoughts.

Red Cross packages began to arrive in December, 1944, with dried milk and sugar cubes! What a feast! Being frugal, I hid some sugar cubes in a tiny box on my bunk.

One night, my hunger nagging me without mercy, I reached up to sneak a cube to suck on when suddenly a hand stabbed through the darkness and grabbed my wrist. A voice demanded, "Who's that?" It was Marga, protecting my cache from a likely thief. My sister and I shared the bunk, with each one sleeping on her side, an arm and leg dangling over

**Lincoln Christian College**

*46763*

the rim. We still touched, with my head keeping company with her feet and vice versa.

It was a real blessing to share a bunk with Marga, for most slept with strangers. You couldn't help but kick each other during the night which added real misery to most lives. Mother had a difficult time with this, for even the sick shared the narrow bunks.

*Christmas, 1944.* The Germans were victorious in a battle, so through their wonderful generosity gave us a great meal. Noodles! The first solid food we had had in a year!

By this time I was very weak and father came to see me. He eyed the noodles, a real treat, and said, "Are you sure you can eat all of that? Are you sure?" The poor man thought he could have some of it, but I was terribly hungry too. It would have taken too much from me to give this unexpected banquet away.

I was perched on top of the third level of bunks. Completely drained of any strength, it was no longer worth it for me to expend the energy required to tediously climb down and get my soup. This was a common sign for the beginning of the end, when slow starvation gradually conquered your body.

Day after day. Night after night. Staring at a gloomy ceiling from my bunk. Luckily it was not long until Marga's work assignment ended and she could take care of me, spooning soup into my mouth and trying to make me comfortable.

Before her job ended Marga was hit with a 104° fever, the minimum you needed to see a doctor. I gathered my inner strength in one piece and took her to the hospital where Marga collapsed in the waiting room. She was relieved of work for two days.

Washing in the bathroom one day I was interrupted by a deafening noise followed by screams of panic and fear from the others in the barrack. I felt something on my head.

I ran outside and immediately ducked under the presence of an airplane zooming low over our building, spraying bullets through the entire area. It was either the Royal Air Force or the Americans.

Hot lead poured through the roof from the machine guns and killed two persons. I ran to father for a mutual checkup and then went to mother. After I was sure the family was intact I touched the top of my head and felt blood oozing from a shrapnel wound. It wasn't serious, but even today when walking or driving my car I instinctively slow down when an airplane flies overhead.

The Allies didn't know it was a concentration camp, but were merely going for an ammunition dump we found out later was hidden somewhere at Bergen-Belsen. We didn't blame the Allies for the attack. All were glad they were still at it. This is part of war.

Bergen-Belsen was about fifty miles from Hanover in the southwestern part of Germany near the Dutch border. When the bombs exploded and fighting broke out in Hanover we would go outside and loudly cheer every time the Allied planes flew over. The Germans punished us for this but the discipline wasn't as difficult to endure as was the sadness of seeing a friendly plane shot down.

Each time a plane flew close to camp an air raid siren wailed. This also meant we would have to take the laundry down because white could be seen from the air. (This may not impress others very much, but it was a whole new affliction added to life.)

It wasn't always easy to find an empty line. The barrack was devoid of any space to hang up clothes. The freezing weather outside picked on our wet laundry and stiffened it if left out too long. I'd wash the clothes, hang them up after waiting for a line, go inside, hear an air raid signal, go outdoors and take down the laundry, go inside, wait, go outside to hang up the clothes again and repeat the entire process. Often I spent all day with the wash.

It had to be done. You couldn't run around in dirty clothes.

On a Thursday night I sleepily nudged Marga in our bunk and informed her the next day was Friday —my lucky day. I'd pray from one Friday to the next that something would happen to free us.

Friday morning Marga went to the washroom, which is like a village marketplace. We called it the JPA—Jewish Press Agency—although the "news" was almost exclusively rumor rather than fact since little outside information leaked in.

She returned to our bunk and said our group of South American passport holders had been called for processing out of camp. This had happened before many times. We'd go for an interview, stand there, and nothing came of it. When the call came those who worked were told to stay in their barrack.

"See, it's Friday!" I told her. "This is going to be it!" It was January 19, 1945.

Marga disappeared for a while, then returned with more news. "Mother, Eric and I have been called— but not you or father."

"Don't worry, we will!" She was worried about it, but not me. After all, it was Friday! Just as I knew they'd be at Westerbork for Chanukah, I knew this was it.

People were called for interviews at either 9:00 A.M., 10:00 A.M., 11:00 A.M. or noon. We went at ten. They asked the most ridiculous questions. Once again, I must have looked stupid to people for the German asked me how I would get to America if they let me go.

My mind had been so dulled from physical weakness that I couldn't understand what he was saying. America? Just let me out of camp!

"With a boat," Marga piped up.

"No!" the German answered, "I want her to answer!"

Having my wits sharpened by now, with keen insight into my inquisitor's personality, and having already heard Marga, I fired back my well-chosen answer:

"With a boat!"

"Good!"

I don't remember any other questions.

Our relatives in America may have influenced their decision. Mother's brothers and Eric's parents and sister had all left Germany before the war and gone to the United States.

Saturday we heard final confirmation about the group which had been interviewed at 10:00 A.M., Friday.

We were leaving Bergen-Belsen. Freedom had barely nipped death at the finish line.

CHAPTER TEN

# Even Exchange

A doctor had to approve our physical status in order for us to travel. None of us was well enough, but Eric managed to spread his hand behind mother's back and support her so she could walk past the physician.

The doctor didn't believe father could make it to the train. He was taken to camp weighing a robust one hundred and eighty pounds. Leaving Bergen-Belsen father was a faint shadow of his old self—a scant seventy pounds remained. They let him go.

We returned to the barrack Saturday night and found all of our blankets had been taken. First come, first serve. The others knew we were leaving and so grabbed whatever they could. We understood, but froze all night.

Sunday morning mother fainted in the shower. She was carried out and revived. Then, for the second time during our stay at Bergen-Belsen, they gave us "good" food: sauerkraut and potatoes.

"Now that they're giving us good food they're sending us away!" mother complained. She didn't want to go! Mother wanted to fight leaving because that one time we had decent food.

We explained to her the food was given to us because we were being sent away, and the rest of the camp still had to manage on the soup and bread diet. She wasn't convinced.

Rumors had circulated before that transports similar to ours had actually gone to worse camps rather than to freedom, so there was no positive assurance we'd get out safely. Mother figured if the food was good now, why take a chance?

The entire time at camp we had to wear our yellow badge, and woe to the person whose badge was loose or—we shuddered at the thought—missing. Who else could we be? There were only Jews there, and a badge wasn't necessary for ethnic identification. It was simply harassment.

The badges were checked on our way to the train. Standing before the cars we heard a long speech threatening us if we told about camp conditions for the arm of the Third Reich was long. No one felt like shaking hands good-bye.

Once on the train the Red Cross took over. There, they gave us the best food possible for starving passengers: a very light bouillon soup with healthy vegetables swimming in it. We found out we could have seconds so we really had a feast.

After about two days the train stopped and they read names of about twenty-five people who had to get off. Most expected certain death at another camp. A terribly sick man, flirting with death for weeks, had remained alive because of an inner will to live nourished by Marga's optimism. When his name was read he died instantly.

Those getting off were transferred to another camp and all survived, but we had no way of knowing this. The Germans announced they needed another to take the man's place and someone suggested Eric. The guard looked on his list and said no. We don't know why.

Less than one hundred of the one hundred twenty-five who left Bergen-Belsen in our group made it across the border. We were part of an exchange: one thousand Americans for one thousand Germans. There were only nine hundred North Americans left in Germany, so they threw in some of us with South American passports to make up the difference.

About half of the four thousand persons in our part of camp had similar passports. We might have been members of this select one hundred people because our friend in Sweden had our papers legalized. The only thing I know for sure is that the Lord was in it.

I wondered just why the Lord helped us get out. We weren't even good Jews while others, wonderful Orthodox Jews with a zealous love of God, were killed. I dwelled heavily on the concepts of life and death. Perhaps death wasn't a punishment after all, that maybe the hearts of many of the Jews killed were right with God.

It's as if God shined down different amounts of His light upon each person, some by experience or circumstance receiving more than others, and He was only interested in holding you responsible for as much light as you had received.

Maybe it was a real privilege to be taken into God's presence by physical death. If this were true then the fact I escaped alive must mean He had a wonderful plan for my life. He had a reason for keeping me.

*January 24, 1945.* The official exchange was made at the Swiss border. We stayed on the same train while they handed us a piece of paper announcing our transfer. A group of German civilians passed us on a train heading in the opposite direction.

Most of the passengers on our train were the nine hundred Americans. They forbade us to come into their cars because we were dirty and full of lice. Then—I was shocked. The Swiss stopped the train and yelled:

"All Israelites go here!"

At the time there was no Israel, only Palestine, and the word "Israelite" carried with it a strong derogatory connotation. They meant it as such. Our clear dreams of coming to a free country were muddied.

They gave us worse accommodations than at Bergen-Belsen. Men, women and children—one hundred of us—huddled in tiers of straw in an old stable. Everyone was sick. Everyone shared one toilet which overflowed within an hour. That left us with no choice whatsoever. It forced us to go into the snow outside and this induced the Swiss to continue calling us dirty names. They couldn't relate to the fact we had just come from a concentration camp, not a ski resort.

They brought us our first meal, a large pail of unpeeled, boiled potatoes. The man who brought it set the pail down, looked away for a second, returned his gaze to the pail and found it empty. He couldn't believe it. The potatoes had disappeared under the straw in a flash. He called us pigs and walked over shaking his head, his well-fed stomach erasing any compassion for starved people he might have had. For us it was different. We weren't sure when we'd be fed again. We saved a potato for evening, but when dinner time came so did another pail. The potatoes from lunch began popping up from under the straw as we grabbed a fresh batch.

After one night my parents and I were taken to a hospital temporarily located in a school.

Four or five days passed before we were to leave Switzerland. Marga, the strong caretaker of the family, called to make sure we were all in good enough shape to travel. When we confirmed that we were she collapsed with typhus.

No one in camp had ever survived typhus fever, a disease contributed by the rampant lice. We were sure this was it for Marga. I'm sure the high fever she had in camp was the beginning, but her strong will kept her walking. Once we were safe she let go, fell apart and was taken to the hospital.

The Swiss, bless their hearts, didn't make anyone travel who was too sick—but they didn't allow any family members to remain with those unable to travel. Some who have said the Swiss knew no anti-Semitism should have been in our shoes. It just wasn't so. Marga had just come from the concentration camp, near death, shaking from her illness and told she'd be left to die with no family present. Our morale sunk to unexpected depths.

As my parents and I boarded the train we searched desperately for Eric and, maybe, Marga. We didn't know what was happening for she was deathly sick and probably wouldn't be allowed to travel. Yet Eric should be there at least, even if Marga couldn't come. We peeked into each compartment, searching for familiar-looking clothes, for a glimpse of her hair or Eric's face. Our train pulled out after a long delay.

Shortly we pulled up to another station where we had to change trains. By this time mother was extremely weak. The doctor said he would help us out, jumped in front of us and led the way to a compartment on the second train.

"Sorry," he said to the people already in that compartment, "but I'm bringing in a lady who's even sicker than you are. You'll have to sit up so she can lie down." Mother had been transferred on a stretcher.

We thanked the doctor and brushed past him into the compartment. The woman made to sit up was Marga! And Eric welcomed us enthusiastically with as much surprise as we felt.

Eric had put up a giant fuss, rearing back on his hind feet and telling the Swiss authorities that either Marga went on the train or he stayed behind. Period! I gave him a lot of credit.

Smiling, crying and laughing, the five "Schlamms" were back together again!

# CHAPTER ELEVEN

# Bomb Hold Evacuation

Eric, father and I took turns standing while mother and Marga extended themselves on the benches. Two of us could manage to sit on a corner near their feet.

The train neared the docks at Marseilles, France. Mother's sweater had been successfully invaded by swarms of lice so she decided to leave it on the train. No such luck. Several persons carried it to us and shouted, "Is this your sweater? Here's your sweater!" We couldn't get rid of it.

As the train slowed, father spotted the *Gripsholm,* a Swedish luxury liner. He had traveled on her before and the very thought of the rich food served on board made him run his tongue over his lips in anticipation.

Father said everything was looking fine and soon we'd be on the *Gripsholm* sailing for America. We were dreaming of hurrying for the ship when another voice of authority cut us short.

"You go over there!"

He pointed to a tiny wooden boat. A far cry from the glory of the *Gripsholm.* Sadly, we walked up a rickety gangplank and onto the boat. It took us farther out in the Mediterranean to a waiting Red Cross boat—an old Italian vessel.

*Gam zeletauvo,* once more for the good, since we wouldn't have done well in America at this point because of the condition we were in.

On board they gave us each one package containing clothes. Mine didn't fit. Don't worry, they advised me, as soon as you get to camp you'll receive new clothes again. With this promise of more to come I returned my package so another could use it.

An American army doctor, on leave, had volunteered his time to take our group across the sea to North Africa. He was a skilled physician as well as being an extremely nice fellow and did so much to nurse Marga back to health that when we arrived she was almost well.

We disembarked in Algeria and were trucked past Algiers to an area near the town of Philippeville. As we approached the camp Eric sighed in disappointment and declared:

"Ah, barbed wire again!"

We learned the wire was to keep out the Arabs, rather than keep us in. It was a U.N.R.R.A. camp— United Nations Relief and Rehabilitation Administration. We were free to come and go from camp and when we did we voluntarily signed out and signed in for our own protection.

Once a week we might take a truck into Philippeville to do a little shopping. There was no place else to go. Our camp was on the side of a mountain, up from the Mediterranean, and another camp was on the other side. You had to travel down the mountain, along the shore and then up again to reach the second camp. It was either this or go across the mountain and risk the danger of Arabs.

The Quonset hut we lived in was divided into small cubicles, with the partitions not quite reaching the ceiling. My parents and I shared a room and finally —after a physical separation of almost two years— Marga and Eric could continue a rudely interrupted honeymoon!

Our stomachs couldn't take the greasy American food we were served. Stews, hash, things like that. We bought much of our own food with money we received from selling our raggedy clothes to the Arabs. If there were three threads left they'd buy it! Later I read accounts of how the Red Cross had gone into Bergen-Belsen with coffee and doughnuts for the survivors. Ridiculous! They shouldn't have offered this type of food to starving people.

The first night at camp we whispered at our table, wondering if we might be lucky enough to obtain a second piece of bread. A man overheard us and returned a moment later with another slice of bread for us. Wow! He was king in our family—so nice to share his bread. Then we found out we could have as much as we wanted.

I remembered the promise made to me on the boat

so I went to pick up new clothes at this camp. They didn't believe my story. "You got clothes on the boat," a woman insisted, "we can't give you any here!" By this time I had only the clothes I was wearing and they were going quickly. I had to beg for every little shirt or sock, which was terrible for me. I didn't like to do that.

Mother was taken to the hospital in the second camp. She went the safe way by the shore rather than chance the cross-mountain trip.

I worked at an administration office located between the two camps at the bottom of the mountain, earning two dollars for a forty-hour week. Typing, filing and general clerical work. One day a man came by with bad news.

"Your father has to go to the hospital too. He's on his way."

I worried, not knowing why he had to go so quickly. The anxiety increased as I sat at my typewriter with nothing to do—not an infrequent occurrence. On many days another girl borrowed my typewriter and I just sat for eight hours. I asked permission to check on my father and they said O.K. He wasn't seriously ill so I returned two hours later for another session of sitting on my hands.

At the end of the week they had deducted ten cents from my salary! Five cents an hour for my time visiting father, but I wasn't doing anything at work anyway! This upset me so much that I quit. If I had only realized this was a typically American practice I wouldn't have taken it so hard.

Everyone laughed at me for constantly wearing a long-sleeved sweater-type shirt. Africa was hot. I was cold. It never impressed anyone I might be sick, even though I had had a bad cough since leaving Bergen-Belsen.

When I first arrived in Algiers the doctor checked me and merely said, "Ah, just be happy and have joy in your heart." It's hard to have joy in your heart when you have a cough in your throat. He thought I was complaining about nothing. The cough continued and I knew I wasn't well, but I stopped complaining because the doctor had said I was fine.

We all gained weight in camp, which we needed, but at the same time my growing feet resulted in badly scraped skin from tight shoes. I had to see the same woman for a new pair of shoes who had previously been so nasty to me in handing out clothes. I asked if I might receive a new pair of shoes at once instead of waiting a week until the scheduled dispersal. It couldn't be done. She stood, told me to soak my feet in cold water, and left.

When mother was released from the hospital I was instructed to requisition a hospital bed and a pillow for her. This same woman was going to give me the bed, but not the pillow. I saw several on the shelves. She raised her eyebrows after I told her it was for mother.

"You know," she said, "you have to get used to normal life again."

It took me a while to understand, then I realized her sarcastic tone reflected a "cleaner," if not superior attitude.

"In normal life," I answered, "we each have a bed and a pillow."

"I hope so."

Because we arrived a snap of the fingers away from starvation, had dirty rags for clothes and only meager belongings, she assumed this mirrored our "normal" life as the scum of the earth.

Yet her husband, the administrator I worked for, was one of the nicest men I've ever met. It's amazing how such different hearts could live together.

President Roosevelt died in April of 1945, and they liberated Europe a month later—signaling everyone at camp to make plans to go to Israel, parts of Europe or America.

Our relatives in America discovered we were still alive by reading the *Reconstruction*, a German-Jewish paper published in New York which listed names of survivors still in camp.

My typing skill led me to become secretary of the group returning to Holland. Our visas for America would have kept us waiting too long so we decided to return to Amsterdam. Eric and Marga could leave for America right away for his parents were there.

Then this supply woman saw me type one day and at once swept my fingers from the keyboard. I might ruin it, even though she knew I had been typing for her husband for several weeks.

At this time a letter arrived from a friend in Holland informing me she had things of mine waiting for our return. Including my typewriter. In my mind I wrote an imaginary letter to this self-appointed pain in my neck at the supply shack:

"Dear Mrs. So-and-so. I want you to know I'm back in Holland in our own apartment, typing on my own typewriter, sleeping in my own bed with my own pillow."

Near the end of our stay in camp they gave everyone a chest fluoroscope. Everyone but me. I asked to be fluoroscoped too, since I was still very sick. They agreed and passed me behind the screen for a split second and pronounced me fit.

*August 30, 1945.* Seven days before our scheduled departure I was running a temperature of 103°. My mother took my temperature again after I begged off a walk around the Quonset hut. It was 104°. I had previously been in the hospital with a high fever and anemia.

A nurse took a quick glance at me, left in a hurry and brought a doctor back within ten minutes. Quite unusual, since physicians were usually summoned from town. They worked on me all night at the hospital barrack in our own camp, waking me every half hour to swallow pills.

This went on for a week before they decided to X-ray my chest again. I was placed in the front of an open jeep, not too clever, and braved the wind during a ride to the main hospital. This time dark shadows appeared on the screen.

"We think there's fluid. Tomorrow we're going to put a needle in." This was on a Friday—not so lucky.

Saturday they put a needle into my chest cavity, constantly changing the bulb of the syringe as it filled.

"Oh, my, so much fluid," the doctor kept saying. This morale crusher was followed by more. He said I had TB. A great comfort to hear when you're thinking about leaving for home. The next morning an American and an English doctor greeted me with ear-tickling grins:

121

"Sorry, you can't go!"

I couldn't take this at all. A sixteen-year-old friend, a nurse's aide, ran to my hut and fetched my parents. They may not have realized how sick I was for they talked the doctors into letting me go. I'm not sure if this was wise or not. Still, the camp was breaking up and I would have had to travel one way or another.

Old meany's husband, now acting camp director, drove mother, me, another woman and her daughter in his private car to the train station. Everyone else went by truck.

Arabs went on and off the train as we endured a miserably long ride to Algiers. All night I tossed and turned on a wooden bench, then transferred to a bed in an Algiers hotel room for five days. While there I overheard Marga coming up the stairs, trying to get Eric to follow her.

"What are you waiting for?" she yelled.

Eric's answer brought a pleasant tingle to my tired body. "Better times!"

At 6:00 A.M. on the fifth day we were taken to an airfield. Marga and Eric stayed behind, then sailed for America and on to Detroit to meet his parents. We were put on a bomber. One recently repaired from a damaging accident. Our group of eight was the first to try it out. The people clustered together where the bombs usually waited for a trip downstairs. The pilot just had to push a button and . . . whooosh!

They attempted to explain, in French, how our parachutes worked. If we had to bail out they would push the button and off we'd go—most likely trying to figure out the parachute instructions on the way down!

I had received a special seat in the cockpit but gave it to a traveler sicker than myself. Huddling in the bomb hold I saw a woman clutch her baby in one hand and a chute in the other. God help her if the hatch opened and she got them mixed up . . . .

# CHAPTER TWELVE

# First Class

There was just one person who got sick on our flight to Lyons, France. Our only nurse. The others managed to hang on.

At Lyons, father deposited me on a park bench for the entire day while he fulfilled his duties as the "wagon master" of our Dutch group, checking on luggage and organizing everyone. He made sure all were on the train before returning for me with just minutes to spare.

"Quick, quick, run for the train! It's leaving!"

"Father, I can't!"

"Run!"

I did my best and we made it. A couple from camp whom I didn't know must have been aware of my sickness for they saved a tiny seat for me in the mobbed train. Better than standing.

We were taken to a repatriation center in Paris, a horrible place where sick, bewildered refugees from scattered camps crowded into limited facilities.

My parents saw the boys who belonged to the family which had had that tiny apartment at Westerbork. Through the Red Cross we contacted their grandmother in Switzerland and told her where they were. She, in turn, told them the location of their mother— and that their father was dead.

The day after we arrived I was taken to a hospital centered in a house. To wash or go to the rest room I had to cross a drafty stairway. I also had to make my bed and get my food, but someone in better shape than I helped me out.

My parents, in their eagerness for me to become well, made a lot of mistakes. They didn't understand that when you're sick, you're sick. They thought if I was up I would be stronger. The doctor didn't care.

"Sure, get up," he said. I didn't feel like it, but logically I decided I had been in bed quite a while so I would leave my bed for an hour each afternoon.

"Get up! Get up!" the nurse said as she threw back my covers. "The doctor said you can get up! Right now!"

I moved to a sitting position on another woman's bed, maintaining this routine for several days. Then my parents wanted me to walk on the street. I did. I admit it's a shame to spend four weeks in Paris and not see the city, but when mother wanted to show me the Arc de Triomphe my sickness didn't complement her enthusiasm.

126

We waited in Paris for The Hague to send us approval to return to Amsterdam. We weren't Dutch citizens, but felt very loyal to Holland. We were with many Dutch people and spoke Dutch at Bergen-Belsen so the Germans wouldn't have the satisfaction of understanding us.

After we arrived in Brussels from Paris, our papers finally in hand, mother and I went to meet her brother at a repatriation center. My uncle was married to a gentile yet had gone into hiding on and off during the war. Father watched our luggage, consisting of several boxes of biscuits and bars of soap. We couldn't use as much as they gave us.

As soon as mother and I walked into the center the front door slammed behind us and a voice vibrated:

"No one can go out today!"

We had just walked into Brussels and were locked up again! I looked through a picture window and saw my uncle coming. The authorities had a transport leaving from Brussels and had shut the doors to eliminate any confusion. At last we convinced them we didn't belong in the group and they let us go.

*October, 1945.* After a day or two with my uncle we boarded a train for Amsterdam. The windows were without glass in our compartment and cold wind whipped through to aggravate my sickness. Then at the Dutch border the officials asked why we had stayed in Paris for four weeks. After all, the papers we had been waiting for really weren't necessary! A perfect case of adding insult to injury.

We had wired ahead to my uncle and others, yet when we pulled into Amsterdam there was no one to greet us. Not a familiar face in a town we called home. I hurried into the office and dialed a number. With each ring my heart threatened to explode in anticipation. No answer. I tried another number, another friend. Always the expectation—always the disappointment. No one answered.

The Dutch at the station were very nice and took us home on a three-wheeled delivery truck. Eric's uncle wasn't there. We waited until about 10:00 P.M. before going to our old building and found our gentile neighbors coming home! The first familiar faces!

When the initial joy had diminished they became a little bit icy in their attitude and said, "We've already talked it over. If you had come with the police we would have thrown all your things on the floor and told you to pick out what belonged to you."

What were they talking about? We were just glad to see them and to be back home. Anything remaining of the things they had kept for us during the war would have been satisfactory. Father had stored a great deal of materials from his factory with them and they had to sell some of it for food. Naturally we didn't expect them to starve while the goods took up floor space.

Their attitude spoiled our reunion. These people were Protestants. Other friends of ours were Catholics. Both had taken their lives in their hands many times during the persecution to visit us and bring vegetables, butter or eggs. The Nazis were "bad" Christians while these people were "good" Christians, for we—like most Jews—believed all gentiles were Christians. One way or another. If I had known how one became a Christian my whole perspective would have changed. This is a hard truth to come by. God in all His wisdom knew it wasn't time to reveal it to me.

Six million of us were slaughtered. Consequently many gentiles who had stored possessions for Jewish friends suddenly found themselves owners of valuable items. One family complained, "We weren't so lucky. All of *our* Jews came back." They didn't mean they were sorry we had returned, just that they hadn't kept things for some who didn't. Either way you swallowed, it left a bad taste in your mouth. Vivid pictures of death in camp contrasted with this attitude of greed created a filthy "welcome home" mat.

Father, having established excellent credit before the war, borrowed about one hundred guilders and started his business again. He was assigned manufacturing quotas, purchased material to make dresses and increased his production rapidly. (Schmidt had taken the business's funds, transferred the shop to his name and kept it going through the war. When the fighting stopped he took the money and fled back to Germany, leaving the machines behind.)

I managed to trace Lore through the Red Cross. She had gone from Vught to Auschwitz and then on to other camps, continuing to do work for Phillips. She was almost killed on a transport to Sweden.

A few weeks after we had settled ourselves in Amsterdam the three of us went to our old doctor for a checkup. It was difficult for me to complete the walk to his office.

Being mostly concerned for my parents, he examined father for his bad heart and mother for her weak lungs. Finding them both satisfactory he turned to

129

me, thinking I'd be the well one. The laugh lines on his face dropped at once. All the fluid in my chest had reaccumulated and he advised me to stay in bed for a few weeks. This was near the beginning of November, 1945.

The "few weeks" lasted until August, 1946. Mother brought me my meals and took care of an inconvenient bedpan as I wasn't even allowed to walk to the bathroom. In May I could make it to the table for meals or could be helped through a quick washing up.

Bed had dominated my world from August, 1945, at Philippeville until a year later. For months and months before that I had been surrounded by people. People everywhere. I couldn't hide from at least one pair of eyes preventing me from spending a few reflective minutes alone. I offered to sleep in the bathtub if others would just respect my privacy.

After I had started to function normally again I went to the synagogue and heard a sermon by our old rabbi in Berlin who had come to Amsterdam. He impressed me by recognizing father right away.

The theme of his talk was love. He said we are not commanded to love our parents, for God cannot command us to love another person. We are only commanded to honor our parents—but *to love God*. This idea remained with me.

A Christian Scientist woman, another baptized Jew, gave me a book by Mary Baker Eddy. I had only been aware of a few of their philosophies, but this book said Jesus didn't want illness, or mean for us to be sick. You were to simply jump out of bed and say "I'm not sick!" I knew this was nonsense. It would be impossible for me to climb out of bed and say "I don't have fluid in my chest" when, in fact, I did. Mrs. Eddy did nothing for my illness yet did manage to cure me of Christian Scientists.

I had refused to go to a hospital when I first became ill again, so this necessitated mother tiring herself out while waiting on me at home. As soon as I was well she had a relapse. After taking care of me for a year, it was my turn to take care of her from 1946 to 1947.

In April of 1947 Lore came to Holland to stay with an uncle and we were together once more.

Meanwhile Eric and Marga were having a rather difficult time in America. He wrote, "You look at monkeys in the zoo and also people in other places." He meant people would stare at these specimens from the concentration camp and tell them how Americans suffered because their sugar and coffee supplies were limited. Marga and Eric weren't too impressed.

Holland had gone through the war, suffering greatly, but certainly not America. The residents of Detroit would apologize to my sister for such things as not having the most up-to-date plumbing. She wasn't even used to plumbing.

Marga had wanted to take a present to her in-laws, whom she hadn't met yet, so she took them the only thing of value she could find at camp—a sack of brown sugar. Eric's mother received the present, picked it up carefully with two fingers and threw it in the garbage.

Eric worked for his father, selling women's gloves, handkerchiefs and other accessories.

During my illness and the following year when I took care of mother I continued taking Spanish lessons and limited most of my reading to books in English. I didn't understand everything but the preparation was very helpful.

I tried to help mother in every way possible, doing errands for her, bringing her anything she wanted and seeing to it that she was comfortable. After spending the morning in bed one day she decided to take an afternoon walk. I was furious. I was happy to help her, but didn't want to see her ruin her health by taking strenuous hikes. When she became insistent this time, I sprinted to the door, locked it and clutched the key tightly in my hand. We fought for it! Wrestling back and forth, mother trying to gain possession of the key. She got a little exercise in spite of me. Afterward mother admitted she was wrong and that I only wanted the best for her.

We started all over again after our arrival in Holland with papers and affidavits in an attempt to obtain visas for America. My parents had grown up in an area of Germany which now belonged to Poland. They were placed in the Polish quota, a much smaller number than the German limit. I could have gone before they could, having been born in Berlin, and I threatened to leave without them if they didn't receive the go-ahead soon. I was anxious to join Marga.

After two years they came through—only because my sister and Eric were already in the United States. Father sold his business in October, 1947, and we sailed on the postwar maiden voyage of the *New Amsterdam*.

First class! Father was only allowed to take a limited amount of money with him so we spent the surplus on expensive tickets. Movies, games, races, good food and pleasant music made the trip most relaxing. For a few days rough weather tossed the ship about and half of the crew were sick. I don't know where I received my wisdom but I told mother to take deep breaths in and out. She was fine.

New York harbor! I couldn't believe it! America looked beautiful to me as we closed the gap between our ship and the shore. Then immigration officials met us with a small boat and climbed on board.

They took one look at me and began the questions. Once again I must have appeared to be stupid for they asked if I could read and write. I smiled victoriously. "In which language?" That cured them! They asked how many languages, already showing surprise I knew English. I added German, Dutch, French and Spanish and they were satisfied.

The passengers elbowed each other as they rushed toward this land of opportunity. A million thoughts raced through my mind. Was this really a new beginning? What would become of Jutta Vera Schlamm?

A familiar, screaming voice broke my mental trance. My eyes roamed the waiting crowd before zooming in on my frantically waving girl friend from Berlin.

Marion!

# CHAPTER THIRTEEN

# The Melting of a Ten-Year Ice Cube

Marion had been sent on a children's transport from Berlin to London, where she spent the war as one of many "daughters" kept in English homes. In actuality they were servants. Two of my cousins who did this were so affected by their chores that today one refuses to cook and the other won't scrub a floor!

Marion had shined shoes. She had arrived in New York six months before our November 6, 1947 docking date. We yelled at each other, hugged and cried after a ten-year absence. Marion showed me New York during the following week and we also visited my cousins from Berlin and Eric's uncle and aunt. I was overwhelmed by the city. By America. And what I might be able to accomplish.

In Europe I heard the United States allowed you to work during the day and attend school at night—something we had never been able to do. I was determined to make something of myself. A dream of securing a fruitful vocation attracted me much more than the vague thought of marriage. I never had really been attracted to any particular boy. Too many years were spent with only survival in mind. I never even imagined I might have a boyfriend—and neither did my family.

My friends said I dressed funny, just like a little girl. I never realized this. My extreme shyness and complex about being so petite added to my romantic isolation. Europeans have a very unusual attitude toward shortness, but as soon as I arrived in America it disappeared as a subject for ridicule.

I wrote to Lore, admitting how sad I was that we only spent six months together before splitting up again. I pleaded with her to follow me to America, but her heart was set on another land of great opportunity. Palestine. After she arrived in the Jewish homeland Lore was married.

Our vacation was over as we headed for Detroit and, once there, ended a two-year wait by celebrating a family reunion with Eric and his pregnant wife Marga!

We went to Chicago to visit mother's relatives for a while, feeling secure that Marga's due date was far enough away so we could return in time for the event. Peter had other ideas! He wouldn't wait and insisted on being born prematurely on November 29, 1947. The same day the United Nations voted for the partition of Palestine! Right off we knew we had a bright little *mench* ("human being"/person) in the family.

The news of Israel's own birth brought almost as much joy as Peter did. When we were in Holland a remote relative had come back from the Middle East and described how difficult it was to develop a barren country where Arabs constantly attacked you at the same time they cried to the world for peace.

I was considering possibilities for training in various areas when Peter's practical nurse told me I could attain her status within one year. She advised me to go to a home near Detroit, sort of a combination orphanage and "child depository" for sick parents. It sounded great. In twelve months I could have a solid profession and at the same time take courses and work with children, something I always enjoyed doing.

After a few weeks in America I found myself at a Catholic home. It had long halls with separate cottages for family units, and looked quite attractive. Twenty children were being cared for in each unit. Another girl and I were not only assigned the task of mothering the children but were also responsible for cleaning the halls, playroom, two locker rooms, four bedrooms and six baths. We spent most of our time with mops and brooms, and watched sadly while the children were shoved around and slapped.

I hated it. After two months they had hired enough Catholic girls for the positions, so my co-worker (a Protestant) and I were fired. They knew I was Jewish. This was the first inkling I had ever received that perhaps there was a difference between Catholics and Protestants. A big difference.

137

*Gam zeletauvo.* The good which came from this was in the form of a better command of English and another name! No one could pronounce "Jutta," my first name, which sounds like a short "Utah." So I began using my middle name. At five in the morning my roommate would call out "Vera" and I sleepily looked for a third person before realizing *I* was Vera!

I certainly didn't mind leaving the home, but it wasn't easy for the children and me to tear ourselves away from each other. We had established a wonderful rapport. I would watch kindergarten teachers come in and work with my little friends and concluded this was really a wonderful profession.

For ten years, from age fifteen to twenty-five, I was placed "on hold." I didn't grow physically or emotionally. A day-to-day existence, a state of being without developing, frozen into a ten-year ice cube which finally melted under the American sun.

After the thaw I only knew I didn't want to be my father's secretary the rest of my life. Other than that I didn't know. I explored the possibilities of becoming a kindergarten teacher. Eric's aunt made an appointment for me at the local board of education. They said to see the people at Wayne University, now Wayne State University in Detroit.

Mr. Cieslak, an extremely likable man, asked about my previous education. Marga helped me figure out how many hours I had had in each subject before our arrest by the Germans. Mr. Cieslak nodded his head.

"You lack three years of high school."

I knew this. Instead of giving up on me he asked me to take an entrance examination at Wayne, for counseling purposes. And on my card he wrote in giant letters: FOR GUIDANCE ONLY.

Not knowing what they would ask, I crammed American history and algebra into my head. But the test wasn't like that. We had to read a passage on one side of the paper, turn it over and within a time limit answer questions about what we had just read. Mr. Cieslak later flashed the results in front of me.

"We'll take you!"

I was stunned. The "guidance" test turned out to be my ticket to enter Wayne in September, 1948, as a special student heading for kindergarten! I needed a "B" average my first year in order to continue in school.

My most difficult class was in English, for although I knew grammar and spelling my vocabulary was poor. I told the instructor I should have been placed in an easier class but she disagreed. My weekly themes came back with written comments of "poor sentence structure" or perhaps "poor usage" scrawled across the top. After six weeks my friends suggested I drop the course, but I wasn't going to give up all that invested time.

One day I was conferring with the instructor in her office about a theme I had rewritten when she asked how I was doing in school. I said very well—except for her course.

"You're doing fine," she corrected me, "passing work. I thought it would be good practice for you to write your theme again since others had to."

She really made me work. My paper would have an "A" scratched off as a grade with a "C" replacing it. "Too bad this paper has to be downgraded because of poor wording," the note would say. I received a "B" in the course. The foundation I had established in English was of tremendous benefit later on.

In mathematics class my hand always shot toward the ceiling when the professor asked for an answer. If possible he'd call on someone else. Once I was at the blackboard, showing at what point a bicycle rider would be met by a man driving a car if the car left at a later time. The professor agreed I had obtained the correct answer, but my "European" methods of approach were so bizarre that at one point he fell off the bike and lost me! He once told another student: "You're just like Vera. She gets the answers but I don't know how!" He couldn't follow my reasoning at all.

During a test in my survey course in physics and astronomy the professor peeked over my shoulder and cautioned me to "Watch your decimal points." What was a "desmal" point? I didn't know. He must have thought I was crazy to have literally missed the point of the problem. He had a lot of fun with me, especially when the word "optical" escaped me for a moment and I wrote down "optional illusion."

I earned better than a "B" average my first year and therefore became a legally accepted American college girl. Six months later someone mentioned there was a height requirement to become a kindergarten teacher. I asked the dean of education if this were true and he said, "If you have to ask about it, maybe you better not go into it." This struck me as being a rather insensitive remark. My entire life I was always too short for this or that and had become very shy regarding the subject. I probably blushed as I asked him.

It was the best thing that could have happened. Being kicked out of kindergarten at the age of twenty-six forced me to take a series of "interest" tests. They indicated science. Of all the things I could choose from I picked medical technology, in order to become a lab technician. I switched my major to biology and minor to chemistry, wondering if I'd like either one. I did.

This entire time I had been working for father in his business of wholesale blouses. He dictated in German and I translated his letters into English rather than Dutch. From my salary I paid board to my parents and tuition to Wayne University.

Father's problems followed me home from his business in the afternoons. Poor times had made father very nervous and it began to wear off on me. Finally I told him to get someone else and I took a job at sixty cents an hour filing stencils at school in the afternoon. I was never replaced at the business, so wound up having to write letters and do bookkeeping at night besides my homework.

In December, 1950, I baby-sat for Peter at my sister's place while she and Eric visited the growing state of Texas. Eric wanted to change his work. In April, 1951, father sold his business and my parents joined Marga and Eric in running a motel they had purchased in San Antonio.

For me there was no other school than Wayne. I had already applied for the school of medical technology for my last year of study.

I wasn't used to regular hours when I had baby-sat

for Peter. I came at any time, so unthinkingly I made the same arrangement with a woman regarding her three children. She'd supply me with a room and I'd be an on-call baby-sitter. My money for food came from my afternoon filing job. Then from 5:00 P.M. on I worked at home taking care of children aged one, three and four years. It was 9:00 P.M. before they were all fed, washed and in bed. I was exhausted. My grades dropped from As and Bs until, after three or four months, they settled during summer school to uncomfortable Cs, something I wasn't used to.

Father wrote me from Texas, offering me a room. I was ripe for a change so gladly packed my bags and joined them in San Antonio.

I considered spending my senior year at the University of Texas at Austin, but the doctor said father's heart condition was so precarious it might not be wise for me to live seventy miles away. In September, 1951, I enrolled as a senior at Trinity University in San Antonio, making arrangements with a local hospital to receive practical training as a lab technician.

Trinity is connected with the Presbyterian Church and two courses in religion were required. The school's chaplain taught both my Old Testament and comparative religion courses. He was excellent. Often he would bring the Old Testament to life by acting out certain characters. At first I thought he had missed his calling, but then realized this histrionic ability just added to his effectiveness as a teacher.

Once a student was heckling him about his belief in creation rather than evolution. He stated he felt it took a great deal more faith to believe we somehow made a giant, unknown leap from a primitive monkey than to believe God breathed His Spirit into us. Then he said something which etched itself on my soul.

"You can't go wrong if you're looking for the truth. And there's only one Truth."

During our comparative religion course we came to Christianity. The chaplain said If Jesus didn't really live, then millions of people have believed a lie. This stirred me up a little, but not much. After all, couldn't millions of people easily believe a lie?

Then he quoted Scripture where Jesus had claimed over and over to have fulfilled Old Testament Messianic prophecy as being the only Son of God. Once more, this "good" man who preached such "good, moral" things was either a raving lunatic or—just who He said He was. This was a little harder to handle.

I became greatly frustrated when my science course across campus ran late and I couldn't run to the chaplain's class quick enough to hear his opening prayer. I was fascinated with what he said.

Prayer had had such dramatic results in my own life that I couldn't discount its power. I had always believed every word uttered from the prayer book in synagogue, even during the persecution in Amsterdam when we were constantly threatened with the possibility of soldiers smashing down the temple door and carting us off.

I had finished my survey courses at Wayne so only had to complete upper-division chemistry and biology courses at Trinity. I was thrown in with the pre-med majors since it was a small, four hundred-student school. Today they have at least twenty thousand.

A girl with whom I studied was also encouraging me to go to medical school with her. Insanity! I had never hoped even to attend college, much less graduate school. I politely declined. Yet the very thought of it began to shift around my desires. My parents had thought I was mildly mad to attend Wayne University.

My friend took me to meet her husband, a dentist, and he suggested I obtain a loan and repay it when I finished medical school. The next day she informed our biology professor, head of the pre-med committee, of her intentions and my stubbornness. He, too, thought it was a great idea.

That clinched it. This was the beginning of 1952. I was long overdue to take a medical aptitude test in order to be admitted that September. I was a girl. I was Jewish (they had a definite quota of Jewish students). I wasn't yet a resident of Texas. I could just barely afford to attend a state school.

But I applied. With everything against me.

# CHAPTER FOURTEEN

# Religiously All Right

The applications were sent to the University of Texas Southwestern Medical School in Dallas and U.T.'s campus in Galveston. As I waited I told Marga:

"If God wants me to go to medical school I'll be accepted. In spite of the odds. If He doesn't I'll continue with my medical technology training."

We had been attending a Reform temple in San Antonio because we liked the rabbi. Although other worshipers really didn't believe a great deal, I continued to feel confident the Bible was the Word of God.

Eric was upset at first that men in the Reform temple didn't wear *yarmulkes,* or skullcaps. I agreed with him. If they want to be Reform and read the prayers in English, OK, for often they displayed more reverence than in Orthodox synagogue. But why did they have to mimic the gentiles and not wear caps?

The rabbi asked Eric to show him in the Bible where it says you must wear a hat. For that point he referred to the Bible. I asked Werner, an Orthodox friend in San Francisco who was one of the boys we had met at the repatriation center in Paris. Where were men ordered to wear caps? He said in Scripture priestly garments included a hat, or head covering, and all Jewish men are priests before God.

My increased contact with questions of God fired me back to an earlier reflection after leaving Bergen-Belsen: My conviction God had a plan for my life. When this question of medical school blossomed I thought that's it! God wanted me to serve mankind. He wanted me to be a doctor.

He did! Southwestern accepted me. I didn't bother to notify Galveston of my acceptance to Southwestern since they had already told me I wouldn't be considered until I became a Texas resident. On the exact day I became a resident, Galveston sent me an acceptance, but I had already prepared for Southwestern.

Language was a problem for me at medical school and I indirectly experienced anti-Semitism. When the girls at Southwestern asked me to join their sorority I told them I was Jewish, because during college there were distinct gentile and Jewish sororities. They extended a quick, friendly acceptance. Yet other students would speak in front of me about the Jewish people.

One Jewish student, a very poor student and disliked by most, would be talked about in nasty terms and ridiculed. It was said he would make it through because many of the professors were Jewish and blood was thicker than water. He didn't!

The faculty advised us female students to mix with the boys during class and not segregate ourselves. Once ten boys and two of us girls lived at a veterans' hospital in seclusion for three months. We didn't particularly like the others, so Valerie and I decided to stick together on the same ward if possible.

The twelve of us were split into several groups, each group under the guidance of a doctor. We saw the doctors flip a coin and the loser was penalized by having to teach the two girls. This made for a very nice beginning!

Between my freshman and sophomore year of medical school I learned to drive and a year later owned my first car—a necessity at that time.

In 1953 I obtained something I had lost almost twenty years before. National citizenship! I had to wait five years. I came prepared for the questions they would ask me which usually concerned a few facts on American history.

When the examiner discovered I had finished a year of medical school he decided to shake me up and tighten his approach.

"Give me the history of the United States."

"Where do you want me to start? Columbus or the *Mayflower*?" I gave him numerous dates and a short sketch of American history. It wasn't easy, but finally I earned my naturalization.

Eric left the motel in 1954 when business slumped and accommodations became too small for his family. Father stayed on but couldn't manage to sell the business. Eric, still ambitious, began working his way up the managerial ladder in a Texas department store.

Summers, after my sophomore and junior years, I worked as an extern in a private San Antonio hospital. The same hospital I had picked for my medical technology training.

An extern works as a doctor while still in training. I was in charge of the emergency room all day long and many evenings. Weekends I was in control of the hospital and was responsible for putting tubes down throats or starting intravenous feedings. These were private patients under the care of their own doctors, any of whom I could call at any time for consultation. Everything I did was ordered by a regular physician.

This was my first practical experience. I had just finished a course in how to perform a physical examination. Now I discovered *interpreting* the results was a different story!

For my first ten days I observed the out-going interns. One fellow taught me how to suture a wound. He demonstrated by letting me sew up a crease in an old hat! Being very ambitious I stayed with him all night while he was on duty.

At midnight a man came in with a stab wound in his arm. The intern allowed me to suture the torn flesh, stopping by every so often and saying:

"You're doing a wonderful job. Just fine."

I responded well to this kind of compliment, for if he had said "how terrible" it might have ruined my whole medical career! The patient, upset from the wound and the aftermath of a fight, didn't seem overly concerned with who was working on him.

The summers gave me a great deal of confidence. Many times patients would come to the emergency room to be treated for things which, with common sense, they could have treated themselves. That's how I treated them. With common sense. I would look in my book and find out what to give for a cough or stomachache. A woman obstetrician was very nice to me and allowed me to help with several deliveries.

When new interns arrived it opened up more parties and good times. We had lots of fun together and they taught me a great deal about medicine.

My second summer I was a little more scared, for I knew more and could better ascertain how much I *didn't* know. Yet the practical experience was invaluable, for even in my junior year, when we were supposed to observe the seniors delivering babies, I knew more than my elders.

I applied for internship during my last year, feeding my preferences to a computer which also gobbled up information from hospitals listing their preferences for interns.

My mother's brother had moved to California and mother wanted to move also. She encouraged me to intern in California. I didn't want to go for I was always loyal to the school or state where I was. First Michigan, then Texas. Yet I applied at two hospitals in San Francisco, the University of California and Children's Hospital in Los Angeles.

I alternated hospitals on my preference list with Los Angeles mentioned, then San Francisco and so on. I couldn't decide on a city. I finally accepted an internship at U.C.L.A. for a straight pediatrics internship rather than a rotating internship covering different specialties. From the beginning I had just wanted to work with children.

In my last year in Texas a very good heart specialist, who knew what he was talking about, argued with me when I wanted father to have a hernia operation. I asked him why not and he replied, "He doesn't have five years to live. Why do you want to bother the poor man?"

This upset me very much. Father wasn't a statistic to me.

My family and friends joyfully celebrated my graduation from medical school in June, 1956, and we spent the evening with good company, good food and good wishes.

My parents fell asleep at about one in the morning as I drove home. My own eyelids were drooping with heaviness when suddenly the white line kept flashing at me. I tried everything to stay awake but discovered I was on the left shoulder of a two-way highway traveling against traffic. Headlights blinded me from the opposite direction. I jerked the car hard to the right and the other vehicle skimmed past. God's hand must have been directing traffic.

Two months after I had moved to Los Angeles my parents arrived from Texas and we shared an apartment together. After our decision to move they were able to sell the motel quickly, something they had attempted for many months.

This same year of 1956 brought Peter a baby sister, Debbie.

My internship was profitable and very enjoyable.

Miserable hours, working every other night and through the next day, but enjoyable. My patients and I became good friends!

A year later I finished my internship at U.C.L.A. and moved June 30, 1957 to Children's Hospital to begin my two years of residency. I brought my clothes to one of the small apartments provided for us.

My assigned room was hot and dirty when I walked in. Not having a chance to clean it that night, I went home and returned the next morning. As I entered one woman was standing in the room and another was still in bed.

It was Le Claire, a girl I had gone to school with at Trinity and who had attended Baylor Medical School. Although we wrote once or twice a year and I knew where she was interning, I had no idea she was headed for Children's or interested in pediatrics. The other woman was her mother. Le Claire's assigned roommate had also brought a friend the night before so they decided to use my apartment. I was startled that Le Claire wasn't as surprised to see me as I was to see her. Laughing, she admitted looking into the closet and seeing my name on the uniforms.

We arranged to room together for the next two years. Le Claire's boyfriend, now her husband, and I called each other "roomie" for I was as likely to find him there as his girl friend. He used our table to spread out his books and study.

After dating several people I narrowed the field down to two. I didn't like it this way, but others said dating two boys at once was all right as long as you didn't have an understanding with either one. It worked out very well. One took me out on weekends and the other during the week.

I preferred the weekend date, realizing it wouldn't develop into anything serious. He was a Jewish engineer and an atheist. Deep down in my heart I knew it would never work. I believed in God. So should my husband.

He took me skiing, something I hadn't done since my youth. After three different outings I promised myself the next time we went I would try the rope tow. Climbing up slopes was an unwelcomed waste of energy!

I thought this would be the next winter, but it turned out to be just a week after our last trip. There was still snow on Mount Baldy during the last week in April when we went. I used the rope tow twice and did fairly well. I was very tired and still a little afraid, yet told myself my attitude was ridiculous. One more time for good measure.

As I grabbed the rope my skis spread out to each side and I fell forward. Wait! Weren't you supposed to fall backward if this happened? Smash! Too late. I broke my leg. Sitting in the snow, my skis tangled beneath me and sparks of pain shooting back the message to my brain, I heard the first words of human sympathy reach my ears.

"Get out of the way!"

I couldn't budge until a man removed my skis and I dragged myself to the side. The ski patrol came but wasn't too convinced my leg was broken. They had heard that a million times.

"Stand up."

For once I was smart and refused. They splinted it for me and took me to a small building for genuine sympathy and hot coffee. The only pain killer they had was aspirin, a powder I'm allergic to.

My friend's Volkswagen wasn't capable of taking me back with a painful leg, so others gave me a ride to town. They were very amused when I asked to be taken to Children's Hospital. They didn't know I was a resident doctor there.

Once back at Children's I wrote my own X-ray request. I waited, then heard the report after the X-ray technician had developed the film. "You're not going to walk on this for a while."

I had a good spiral fracture of both leg bones. When the anesthesiologist found out I had eaten part of a candy bar on the way down the mountain he was afraid to give me a general anesthetic. Morphine and a sedative did the trick beautifully.

I opened my eyes in the operating room after they had properly set my leg, still woozy from the drugs, and saw a crowd of laughing faces smiling down at me. I fell asleep. The next morning when I woke I glanced at my cast and found "I told you so!" written boldly on the plaster.

My boyfriend who had taken me skiing felt sorry I had broken my leg, feeling slightly responsible, so he did a very gentlemanly thing to ease his sense of guilt. He proposed. At first I was very excited, and naturally thought we would be married. I had been praying for God to somehow bring our relationship to some kind of conclusion.

It concluded. Five days after we became engaged! Oh, well. It was short but sweet. We both changed our minds, but he was the one who actually broke it off. I was too chicken. We had only known each other for three or four months.

It was a little upsetting to break up with him just when I needed someone the most. My other regular date, the one everyone liked, took me for rides and helped take my mind off the cast. He was quite popular with my girl friends, my parents and me—but I didn't want to marry him.

One day he called me and mentioned he had gotten engaged! He was dating another without my knowledge. I smiled happily at Le Claire when I told her the news.

"You sure look happy about it!"

"I am. Now the pressure's off."

The hospital knew my situation step-by-step as personal news had a way of exploding from the most well-kept sources. Once when I called the switchboard and asked for an outside line the operator congratulated me for having stood up with crutches for the first time.

During my last year at Children's I spent two months at Orange County Hospital as the only resident pediatrician in charge of several interns. When an emergency hit us at Children's all the chiefs came to the powwow and we Indians just stood by. At County I made the decisions.

I did everything. A fifteen-month-old child was brought in dying from meningitis. I fought hard to save his life, in spite of an intern asking me why I made such a tremendous effort. I told him the child was healthy, with no brain damage, so he deserved a good fight. We won.

Another child came in with severe jaundice and I lost track of the number of transfusions I had to do day and night. By the time I was through with him sheer exhaustion had unplugged a fountain of tears. My cheeks were soaked as I walked home. I stumbled along, thinking only of sleep. Precious sleep. During the day county prisoners worked in the hospital laundry. At night I slept above the laundry floor in an old apartment. As I entered downstairs I heard a man's voice coming from my place. No one else lived in the area. Too tired to be scared, I called up and asked who it was. The "voice" identified himself as a doctor. (The resident who had had the apartment before me had given a key to this man who often stayed there after working late at the hospital. Other residents rented a house on the beach at Balboa, working normal hours at the hospital. I didn't know how they did it. I was never off.)

The "visiting" doctor was shaving as he began to lecture me on the foolishness of working so hard that I became physically enervated. I just wanted to sleep. He said to take it easier. I stared at my bed, the chair, the floor, anywhere. I had to sleep. "It's unnecessary to tire yourself out like that." Sleep, sleep. "Furthermore I think you . . . ." He finally left and I collapsed.

During my residency I seriously investigated my faith. God often dominated my thoughts through camp, college and medical school. I went to services as often as I could, especially on the High Holidays.

I admired Le Claire for being a faithful Catholic. She went to mass and answered a lot of questions for me about her religion. Yet when she asked certain questions about Judaism I couldn't always answer. This encouraged me to learn more.

I told her I didn't need to confess my sins each week as she did since I did this once a year on Yom Kippur (Day of Atonement). After I had confessed all my sins I felt forgiven.

I had always read the translations of prayers in synagogue and meant them. That's a big difference for most. You can read them, or you can mean them. As soon as I told Le Claire I had felt forgiven after reading a list of my sins on Yom Kippur I began to wonder about it. I always knew I would be committing the same sins I had just asked forgiveness for.

I never intended not to commit them. To keep the Sabbath the way it should be kept or maintain the dietary laws were quite impossible for me, and these were the two areas I was most concerned about.

Even when at Bergen-Belsen I asked father if we might not be more Orthodox when we got out. Even though I felt many observances were traditional I admired the Orthodox for trying.

On scattered weekends I would fly to San Francisco and spend a couple days with Werner, my link to Orthodox Judaism. Friday nights we had *kiddush,* a real chicken dinner and then said grace after the meal. I enjoyed this immensely.

Saturday mornings we'd walk to synagogue together, go for a stroll in the park afterwards and then have dinner. It wasn't a dating relationship, I was just good friends with his family.

At home I would often play a favorite record. One song was called "One Way" and the lyrics claimed there are many ways which lead to God, so walk with me, brother. It finished with "your God and my God are one."

This was my philosophy. I told Le Claire she was born a Catholic, I was born Jewish and we each did the best with what we were. After two years of discussing religion, she said, it's amazing how we each had different faiths yet believed the same. The same, because we both wanted to serve God the right way.

I thought I had really scored there and had convinced her I was religiously all right!

As I crawled under the covers to go to sleep I would play another song whose lyrics went something like "Good night, dear Lord, the day you gave me today was bright. Show me the way to do what's right. Good night, dear Lord, I'll see You in the morning. Good night." I loved it.

Another song said something about how they used trees to make benches and things like that, but they also used a tree to make a cross for Him. I had trouble understanding the words. On the other side were *Kol Nidre* (a sacred chant sung on the Day of Atonement) and *Eli, Eli,* two of my favorites. A real ecumenical record!

I also had a copy of Handel's "Messiah." I saw the word "Messiah," thought "that's Jewish," and bought it.

When I was through with my residency and in my own private practice, I promised myself I would take off Friday nights, get my parents to say *kiddush* and then go to temple.

I was determined to find out what Judaism was all about. By reading the Bible. This is a most uncommon method, since most rabbis would recommend one of several books explaining Judaism. All I can say is the Lord made me do it!

It dawned on me that there were similar practices between Orthodox Judaism and Catholicism. Each contained large pieces of man-made tradition in the stew. I didn't like the taste of anything man-made. I only wanted to believe God.

It says in Exodus you are not to light a fire on the Sabbath, Werner told me, so this is the reason we aren't allowed to drive. Because you would be igniting a spark in the engine. It wasn't because of any work involved.

I told him if I couldn't drive on the Sabbath then I couldn't pick up my parents and take them to temple. He said it would be better for them to stay home. Werner's sincerity and love of Judaism could reach me, but this answer didn't make any sense. I thought God would appreciate it more if they came to worship in the temple than He would worry about my driving.

Continually trying to grasp the heart of God, if not formal Judaism, I began to focus in on a life's dream. To explore the land of the ancient Bible. To walk on the ground we helped support in my Zionist youth group. To once again see Lore and my cousin Guenther, whom I hadn't seen in twenty-one years.

Absolutely. I had to visit Israel.

# CHAPTER FIFTEEN

# In the Homeland

I boarded a plane for Tel Aviv in August, 1959, a few weeks after completing my residency. Guenther lived in Haifa, a long trip from Tel Aviv, so I told him not to pick me up.

It was thrilling to arrive in Israel for the first time, as if some long slumbering memory bounced to my consciousness and said this was once home, or soon would be. As I walked down the gangplank I scanned the crowd and recognized a tall, bobbing head.

Lore! Her face was blurred by the distance but that nod could belong to no one else. An older cousin and his family also greeted me, which proved to be momentarily embarrassing since I confused him with his son. He was seventeen years older than I, and Marga and I would call him "uncle" since we couldn't relate to him as a cousin. I hadn't seen him in twenty-four years.

Lore and I took a taxi to Jerusalem. By the time we arrived our twelve years of being apart seemed to melt away, so we felt 1947 was only yesterday. We simply continued where we had left off.

I wrote Guenther, telling him I would come when it was convenient for him. Two days later a telegram in Hebrew came for me which read: EXPECT YOU TOMORROW. That's all. No directions. No address. I only had a post office box which I had been writing to.

How typical of Guenther! This amused me greatly and I told Lore if he expected me the next day then I'd be there! Somehow. Lore put me on a bus for Haifa and told me how to say two things in Hebrew: "How much does it cost?" and "Too much."

I took a taxi from Haifa to Guenther's village of mostly German immigrants—Qirjat Bialik, a twenty-minute ride from the bus station. The driver spoke Hebrew, Russian and a few other languages unfamiliar to me. I spoke German and English but the only common tongue we had was Hebrew—and I knew only a smidgen. He couldn't understand that I didn't know Guenther's address. My cousin was well known, having a good-sized carpentry factory where he made furniture and finished cabinets for homes.

The driver thought I was slightly mixed up and asked me in Hebrew Guenther's mailing address, thereby attempting to extract an address from me. I was stumped. How do you say post office box in Hebrew? At last my memory served me well and I recalled an old address of his he had from before the war. The driver took me there and I entered Guenther's house just as he and his wife Bela were sitting down to eat. Perfect timing!

Bela and I clicked right away. She was delightful, quickly asking Guenther how he had expected me to find them if he hadn't sent directions. He shoved his fork into some food and grinned. He knew I'd make it.

"Is it really you?" Guenther kept saying. "Are you really here?"

I could only stay a few days since Lore and I had arranged to take a trip to Beersheba, Sodom and the Dead Sea. After my trip with Lore I returned for a week with Guenther, then spent a week with Herman, my cousin who had met me at the airport. Each drove me all over Israel, giving me a deluxe tour of many sights.

As a teenager I had been active in collecting money for the planting of trees in Israel. Here I saw what had developed! Remarkable forests and orchards where desert had been ruling for centuries. I was very proud of what the Israelis had accomplished.

Constant references to the Bible also impressed me. They'd say, "This is where David hid in the caves," and so on. I became aware that this really was the land of the Bible, and the things I had read about and stories told to me since childhood had actually happened here! Here! Israel! I was drunk with love for the land.

In Nazareth they brought me to a church and said,

"This is where Jesus was born," or else "This is where He grew up." We really joked about it for it seemed that wherever Jesus stopped for a drink of water or to rest for a few minutes a church would miraculously spring up on the spot.

There's a half dozen churches which say *this* is the spot where Jesus spent his boyhood, or *this* is where He did such and such. This was absurd, since they all couldn't be right. Perhaps none was. They'd have you peek in and see a little niche where Joseph allegedly had his carpentry shop.

At the same time my thirst for what the Bible had to say grew my respect for the Israelis in one aspect shrunk a great deal. They were so irreligious. There's the ultra-Orthodox and the nothings. I wondered if a Reform movement might graft a few practices in Judaism back onto their tough Israeli hides.

When flying to Israel it was a delectable, daylight adventure. On our return flight we managed to zoom just ahead of the sun. You think it's night, so you should sleep, but the alertness of your mind dictates you are refreshed and should be expecting the dawn. It seemed as if most of the twenty-four-hour day was spent inside of a never-ending tunnel of blackness. No end to the night. The proverbial speck of light at the end of the underground channel never appearing. Waiting for a sleeping sun which refused to wake made me feel miserable.

I wondered if perhaps this was just a microcosm of what eternal darkness must be like. Being away from God.

# CHAPTER SIXTEEN

# More Light

I returned to Los Angeles with seven weeks of Israel behind me and a private practice waiting ahead.

Then came the days of locating with a private group of doctors in Glendale, meeting the Palmers, my strange attraction to them, and our knocking heads with Isaiah.

About the beginning of November, 1961, the parents of eighteen-month-old Tommy Palmer invited me to join them for a weekend at Rev. Palmer's brother's house in Lake Arrowhead (a two-hour drive from Los Angeles). My nurse was surprised when I broke a long-standing rule and became socially involved with these patients. She asked why I had accepted.

"Well—they're—so nice!"

What could I say? They didn't have much money, so as we went along I either trimmed their bill or didn't charge them anything. If the Palmers wanted to reciprocate with a favor, why not? What it amounted to, simply, is that I liked the idea of spending the weekend with them. My nurse and her husband joined us.

I didn't know at the time if they knew I was Jewish (which they did), but they mentioned nothing about God during the two days. I told of the concentration camp, just in case they were in doubt as to my ancestry!

My Bible reading was also brought to their attention for I wanted them to realize I, too, was religious. God was discussed only at grace before we ate. A simple thanks. Le Claire's practice of saying grace had indoctrinated me into the ritual. I wasn't uneasy and thought it was a nice gesture.

We became fast friends following that weekend and the next thing I knew the Palmers were at my apartment ready to partake of a hectic meal I had prepared.

When you live alone you're used to speedy snacks, not involved dinners. It was a giant hassle for me. After they were seated at the table I would tell them to go ahead and eat while I finished a couple of things in the kitchen. Then I felt bad for not giving them a chance to say grace.

One time I remembered. I sat down with them, waited, looked from one to the other, and they didn't say it! They thought it might have been offensive to me in my own house. When I related my disappointment to Lisa later on she said, "Oh, I'll tell Milton you wanted to say grace. He'll be so happy about that!"

My first excuse to visit their home came in December. Lisa promised to show me how to make pillows for Christmas presents. I planned on giving them to mother for Chanukah.

While figuring out patterns and threading needles I realized I had a captive minister in the house and maybe he'd be able to answer my questions. I asked Milton how one knew which was the right religion, since you're born into it and you can only do your best to claim whatever benefit you desired from it. He took a split-second to answer.

"I knew when I accepted the Messiah as my personal Saviour."

Astounding! I had always believed religious Jewish boys became rabbis and religious Christian boys became ministers. I had no idea a man like Milton could accept the Lord on a personal basis after becoming an adult and then refer to Him as Messiah.

Then Milton added:

"What happened to the sacrifices in the Jewish religion?"

"I don't know, but I'll find out for you."

"OK."

I thought he wanted information, not knowing the answer.

When I put this question to Werner he explained sacrifices stopped when the Temple in Jerusalem was destroyed. No Temple, no sacrifices. This sounded strange for I thought if God wanted sacrifices He was capable of finding a place to do it in!

Once when I was talking to Lisa, she put the phone down for a second during our conversation and Milton picked up the receiver. "I've been thinking about you, Vera, and feel you should read the book of Luke and book of Romans. Luke was a physician and wrote an objective account, just as you write a medical chart. And there's a great deal of reasoning in Romans, the logic of which is often studied by law students."

What was he trying to tell me? I had let them know very distinctly that I was reading the Bible, always having it in view when they came to visit. Yet, I imagine he had a right to suggest what he did.

Romans was completely over my head. Nothing made sense to me. Many verses in Luke spoke to me, though, especially one which said:

"I came not to call the righteous, but sinners to repentance" (Luke 5:32).

That leaves me out, I thought. I'm righteous. I came across Luke 9:62, "No man, having put his hand to the plow, and looking back, is fit for the Kingdom of God."

Had I put my hand to the plow? I shut the Bible. Luke's account wasn't an eyewitnessed record of events, merely what he had gleaned from others. I took note of this fact, never admitting to Milton I had read either book.

"I read something in the paper today," Milton said frequently. "It reports exactly what is prophesied in Ezekiel." I'd run for my Bible, look up the Scripture, and marvel that in front of me, written thousands of years ago, were tomorrow's headlines!

Sunday afternoon. Sometime in February, 1962. I was visiting at the Palmers, when he asked if I'd like to join them that evening when he preached on the First Psalm. It sounded interesting.

I decided I could worship in church as well as in temple. Besides, I was curious as to what went on inside of a church. Milton, sensing a slight hesitation, read the psalm to me to show how "safe" it was.

"Blessed *is* the man that walketh not in the counsel
    of the ungodly,
 nor standeth in the way of sinners,
 nor sitteth in the seat of the scornful.

"But his delight *is* in the law of the LORD;
 and in his law doth he meditate day and night.

"And he shall be like a tree planted by the
    rivers of water,
 that bringeth forth his fruit in his season;
 his leaf also shall not wither;
 and whatsoever he doeth shall prosper.

"The ungodly *are* not so:
 but *are* like the chaff which the wind driveth away.

"Therefore the ungodly shall not stand in
    the judgment,
 nor sinners in the congregation of the righteous.

"For the LORD knoweth the way of the righteous:
 but the way of the ungodly shall perish."

The message was impressive. Milton vividly described the final end of the godly and ungodly, with the ungodly being chaff in the wind. Chaff, he emphasized, was completely worthless. I figured this is one subject he should know about, since he had owned a grocery store before going into the ministry.

Then he quoted Jesus in John 14:6:

173

"I am the way, the truth and the life, no man cometh unto the Father but by me."

At the close of the sermon I realized he had called me ungodly because I didn't believe in Jesus. I was greatly annoyed. We were friends, and he knew I was Jewish. Why did he have to say that? A good friend calling me chaff in the wind! I said a brief farewell:

"Many happy returns of the day." (It was his birthday.) "You'll have to come to temple with me some time."

"I will."

The words of his sermon nagged me day and night. I couldn't force them from my mind. Every night I swallowed hard, took a deep breath and asked God to show me if Jesus really is the Messiah. It seemed ridiculous, but one way or another I was positive Isaiah was getting a big kick out of me.

Just as I believed it was peculiar to pray to Mary to get to Jesus, I thought it foolishness to pray to Jesus to get to God the Father. All my life I had prayed directly to God and He answered my prayers, giving me a peace which confirmed our personal relationship. I had this Jewish aversion to middlemen.

Back to my Bible and the Orthodox prayer book I had received in 1943. It had survived the years with me and contained an English translation. To take a firmer grasp on Judaism I read the prayer book each morning and evening.

The morning prayers included thirteen articles of faith, which every Jew was supposed to firmly believe and rehearse daily. One said: "I believe with a perfect heart that all the words of the prophets are true." Even Isaiah?

174

The last one said: "I believe there will be a resurrection of the dead on such a day as it will please the Creator." Oh, no! A resurrection in Judaism? Yet here it was.

The book emphasized many prayers regarding righteousness and sin. Prayers which destroyed my earlier appraisal of myself. In part: "Our God, and the God of our ancestors, may our prayers come before Thee, and withdraw not Thyself from our supplications, for we are not so shameless of face, or hardened as to declare in Thy presence, O Eternal, our God, and the God of our ancestors, that we are righteous and have not sinned."

Whoops.

"Verily we confess, we have sinned." The prayer continued to list several assorted sins, then followed with:

"O may it then be acceptable in Thy presence, O Eternal, our God and the God of our Fathers, to pardon all our sins, and forgive all our iniquities, and grant us remission for all our transgressions."

This went on and on for several more pages, indicating the many ways a man could consciously or unknowingly commit sin against God. Every so often it would say:

"Yet for all them, O God of forgiveness, forgive us, pardon us, and grant us remission."

I basically still felt very righteous and that I had not committed any of the gross sins detailed in the prayers. But not keeping the Sabbath nor the dietary laws still bothered me.

For several years I had wondered what it meant to be written into the Book of Life as Jews requested on

175

Rosh Hashana, the New Year; and Yom Kippur, Day of Atonement. People die every day, every year, if not from anything else then at least from old age. Does that mean their prayers weren't answered? Or does the Book of Life refer to life after death?

Werner said we didn't have the same concept of eternity as Christians do. He never explained just what our concept is, but did say we believed in eternal life.

He also gave me a vague answer when I questioned him about a reference in the prayer book to Satan. Werner's answers never satisfied me. Who *is* Satan? What *is* our eternity? I still didn't know. The core of what Werner believed was solid and I respected him for it. I wished my mind didn't constantly try to grasp the fringes of religious insight which stepped beyond the scope of his information.

Early in 1962 I passed the written part of an examination on my way to becoming a board certified pediatrician.

Pediatrics is a general practice in a growing organism, and you must be familiar with every area. My oral examination would be given in the fall.

One of the doctors in our group moved to private offices in another building and encouraged me to join him. March 1, 1962, I followed suit and now share office space with another Glendale pediatrician although our practices are completely separate.

Momentarily pushing aside intellectual, argumentative and confusing probes into the nature of religion I went back to my tried and true method I had always known and just talked to God. I wanted Him to help me with a problem. Losing weight. If I gained a pound it looked like ten, especially in my face. By this time I didn't care about scientific this or that, and so was wide open when Marga suggested a particular diet.

Not that He didn't already know, but I reminded God I had never been able to lose weight on any diet. I made a deal. If I lost weight by following Marga's diet it would be His way of showing me I was on the right track in my search for a greater truth about Him.

I lost so much weight that a colleague warned me not to lose any more.

The Palmers were praying about a possibility he would pastor a church at Lake Arrowhead. Finally he was called and accepted the position, promising to baptize some people at the mountain church on Good Friday even though he didn't begin officially until summer.

My parents were planning a vacation at the lake so I drove up with the Palmers to check out the cabins. (It was during Passover week and I had fixed myself a bunch of *kremsle*—pancakes made of unleavened bread. My gentile friends, the Palmers, gobbled them up in nothing flat! I was flattered they liked them.) We stopped at Crestline, a community below Lake Arrowhead Village on the mountain. Pastor Palmer was using the baptistry at a church here since his future congregation met in a former store building. He explained they were going to have communion service, passing the wine and wafer, and I didn't have to take it. I didn't realize he was telling me *not* to take it.

Each of the eight persons being baptized explained

how they knew they had "Jesus in their heart." I heard these brief testimonies of faith, but before Milton could deliver his sermon the word went out that a baby-sitter was needed in the nursery. I really wanted to hear the message but Lisa was the only volunteer to stay with the children. What right did I have to stay for the sermon if the pastor's wife can't hear her husband during his first official function? I volunteered even though I didn't want to baby-sit. They thought I was trying to escape the service.

It was a pleasant weekend. During the next month, in May, I attended a church-sponsored "mother-daughter" banquet in the afternoon. Lisa said I could be her daughter!

I appreciated the Palmers because they were friends without being concerned one way or another about my being Jewish. Through the years other gentiles would befriend me, overlooking the fact that I was Jewish.

It was the Palmers last Sunday in Tujunga before moving to the lake. I decided to attend Milton's final service which began not too long after the afternoon banquet had concluded.

He gave his testimony. Milton, who seemed to be describing a completely different man, told of how he once drank heavily from early morning until late at night. Lisa said for five years she never kissed him without the smell of alcohol on his breath. Then one day he fell to his knees, asked the Lord into his life and stood up a new man, miraculously delivered from any desire for liquor.

The weekend after the Palmers moved to the lake my parents and I had planned on going up, yet I hadn't received a new address from Lisa during those few days. Another doctor said he heard they lived in Cedar Glen near the lake. I asked where this community was after I arrived, surprised at myself that I would deliberately seek them out. I normally don't hunt people down. It was more like they had a hook in me and were slowly reeling in an invisible line.

The Cedar Glen shopping center had a sign reading: COMMUNITY BAPTIST CHURCH with an arrow pointing the way. I took a chance they didn't live too far from the church and prepared myself for a time-consuming crisscross of all the streets until I spotted their Volkswagen van.

As I drove toward the church Milton stepped through the front door, his face revealing complete astonishment at seeing me. The Palmers, obligated to attend a church meeting the next night, accepted my offer to baby-sit for Tommy. They apologized for not having a place for me to stay if I decided to visit again, but I spotted a tool shed with a bed inside next to their one-room apartment. After Bergen-Belsen I could sleep anywhere. My recommending living accommodations in the shed startled them!

Two weeks later I tried it out. I stayed overnight on Father's Day and, out of courtesy, attended church with them Sunday morning. Whenever they said the name of "Jesus" I would say, *Schma Yisrael, adonai elohaynu, adonai echad:* "Hear O Israel, the Lord our God, the Lord is One." It worked fine.

That weekend I hopped in the car with Lisa when she scooted off to pick up some new stationery. We were so busy talking about religion she missed the store three times! I told her firmly I didn't need Jesus for I prayed to the Father all my life and He always delivered me. I had a direct line to God. Toll free.

She amused me as she kept flying past the store, for I could tell what I was saying was affecting her! After we had returned home she stood rigidly, stared me straight in the eye and declared,

"Vera, the Lord has had His hand on you."

I walked from their tiny home to Milton's office in the church.

"It's really interesting," the minister began, "for I just finished reading a book on Abraham. Just think. God called Abraham and told him to leave his family and step out. And what did Abraham do? He dragged his family along. He went with his father part of the way, then took his nephew. It wasn't until he let his family go that God could bless him."

How could Milton possibly know what was troubling me? Why would he mention this right at this time? How could he know this was a major problem of mine?

He handed me a prophecy edition of the New Testament, with all Scripture in boldface type referring to Old Testament prophecies. There was a prayer in the front of the book which said: "In appreciation of the gift of this Book I will read it, and will pray to God to show me the Truth as I read." Then, on the other side was a simple prayer: "O God of Abraham, Isaac, and Jacob, show me the Truth as I read this Book; and help me to follow the Light that is given me by Thee. Amen." I prayed this as I ventured into the New Testament.

I enjoyed receiving presents, an infrequent event during my youth. Their gifts were always well chosen. The previous Christmas they had given me a hand projector so I could show movies I had taken in Israel.

Still grasping for something I wasn't sure of, when I came back from the lake I speculated that perhaps God had been good to me and answered my prayers, but now He was showing me a new truth and wanted me to accept it. More light for greater vision.

Imaginations of how my family would react to a new belief haunted me, causing tremendous worry. Was I trying to escape? From what? I always said a Jew who changed his religion was trying to escape. Like those baptized Jews I knew in Europe. But somehow they didn't seem like believers. Not like the Palmers.

No, I wasn't trying to escape. Just trying to walk closer to God. But what about the subconscious? Ah, the subconscious! Perhaps mine was simply a case of a mixed-up id! If I had to make that terrible decision it had to be because of what God wanted, ignoring the pressure from family, friends, rabbis, ministers, priests or Mary Baker Eddy.

A week later Milton sent me a letter, thanking me as the new pastor of the church for attending their services and hoping I'd come again. Besides—he wanted to show off his new stationery. He thanked me for spending the night with them even if it was in the tool shed.

This letter left me with a reaction which countered the many hours I had spent reading the New Testament he had given me. Curiosity was one thing, but this was going too far! He knew I only came to church because we were friends.

He had to be told right then I could never in a thousand eternities become a Christian. I would not be a Christian, if that's what he had in mind, *ever*. I wanted to make myself clear. It meant nothing for me to go to church.

I tried three times to write these thoughts down. I couldn't do it. It was too difficult for me to actually say it didn't mean anything to me. I ended my wasteful ripping of stationery by writing that as new pastor of the church I hoped Milton would have time to talk to me the next time I came up.

The same day I wrote Lore and informed her I felt myself being drawn to what I was reading and hearing, but hadn't made any decision.

In a previous letter Lore had written it wasn't fair of the minister to say things like "no man cometh unto the Father but by me." I must have told her he had said you're not godly unless you believe in Jesus.

"You're friends with a Baptist minister?" people would kid me. "They're going to try and convert you!"

"No!" I'd fire back, "they're not! We just share beliefs."

Now for the first time in my relationship with Milton I felt a strong, back-bending push to make a decision. I didn't like it.

# CHAPTER SEVENTEEN

# "God, Show Me"

A built-in alarm clock shook me awake and I reached for the radio. It was 6:00 A.M. Nearly every day, for almost two years, I had begun each morning by listening to the Lord's Prayer being sung. It gently transported me from the twilight zone of sleepiness into thoughts of the day's activities.

Often I would tune in on a radio minister who commented on selected stories from the Bible. I enjoyed the close of his program the most when he gave the benediction.

As I went to Friday night services in temple I heard messages which God used to draw me. I remember two sermons specifically. One, based on Exodus 23:2 ("Thou shalt not follow a multitude to *do* evil") made me wonder whether I was following the crowd rather than going by God's truth. The other, some time in May or June of 1962, used Proverbs 29:1 ("He, that being often reproved hardeneth his neck, shall suddenly be destroyed, and that without remedy."). Was God reproving me, as He was guiding me into new truths? How long would He be patient with me?

Arriving home later one night after a service, I found out one of my patients had been taken to Children's Hospital. As I drove to the hospital I prayed for God to make the baby well. I bit my lip. I would even pray in Jesus' name, if I had to, if this would somehow speed up the child's recovery.

As I entered the room my patient's father greeted me with much surprise, saying he didn't know what happened but as soon as I walked in the child became alert. He had been soundly unconscious. The baby was soon well.

Sporadically—when sitting at my table to eat—I would say grace and quickly add, "Thank You, God, in Jesus' name," just to try it out. I really didn't know what I meant by that.

Saturday, June 30, 1962. A nurse who had joined me at the office a week before drove to the lake with me. She was from Lake Arrowhead and had just become a believer in Jesus. During the trip, shooting along the freeway and then winding up the mountain, she sang "How Great Thou Art." I liked it very much, feeling I could sing it since it made no direct reference to Jesus. After all, even the Jewish prayer book says "God of our salvation."

Milton greeted us warmly and, after the usual stretching to iron out the traveling kinks, he asked if I would like to talk for a while. Even though we were good friends I couldn't separate the fact he was a minister "up there" and I was an ordinary person "down here."

I asked if a Jewish person would have to give up his holidays upon accepting Jesus as the Messiah; and if Christians believe in the Old Testament as he said, then why don't they observe the holidays?

He explained the New Testament is a continuation, a fulfillment of the Old Testament. In Matthew 5:17 this man who claimed to have been the promised hope of Abraham, Isaac and their descendants declared:

"Think not that I am come to destroy the law, or the prophets: I am not come to destroy, but to fulfill."

He said if I still felt a need to observe the holidays after accepting the Messiah then I should. But, perhaps, I might discover that although a sixty-watt light bulb illuminates many truths and hundreds of promises, the glory of a two-hundred-watt bulb far outshines it.

I asked Milton about that "ask and ye shall receive" verse which most are familiar with. I had read "Of Human Bondage" and remembered the man had prayed for his clubfoot to be cured. To me this was horrible. How could someone have taught him to pray like that in the wake of certain disappointment since, as a doctor, I knew a clubfoot was a clubfoot. It didn't disappear overnight. He showed me 1 John 5:14: "And this is the confidence that we have in him, that, if we ask any thing according to his will, he heareth us."

Ah, so that's the catch! "According to his will," it said. I was satisfied. No, wait a minute! Am I not the daughter of God just as Jesus or Milton or anyone else is the son of God? How about that? The preacher flipped the pages and read Galatians 3:26:

"For ye are all the children of God by faith in Christ Jesus."

So be it. Another qualification! Suddenly divergent pieces of the jigsaw puzzle were being pulled together by God's Word and His Spirit. Everything made sense. I told Milton about *gam zeletauvo*, my Yiddish expression which means all things work for the good. Once more he turned to the Scripture. Didn't the Lord forget *anything*?

"And we know that all things work together for good to them that love God, to them who are the called according to *his* purpose" (Romans 8:28).

I was shocked. He hadn't forgotten! After three hours of a spiritual question-answer time in which I saw clearly how God had loved and committed Himself to me, Milton asked the inevitable.

"Do you wish to receive Christ?"

"No."

I had promised myself I wouldn't make a "rash" decision. I had prayed about it for four months, continually seeing His guiding hand and reading the Bible, but wanted to make no rash decision! No pushes, shoves or nudges for me. Milton didn't say another word.

Milton and Lisa went out that evening. As I baby-sat for Tommy I figured he would want to hear a

188

Christian song so I sang "Jesus Loves Me, This I Know," the same one my niece Debbie had sung for Marga!

When left alone at the Palmers I would open their Bibles and look at how nicely marked and colored they were. That night I'd open the Bible, feel terribly uneasy, then slam it shut. Open, shut, open, shut. I left it alone.

I climbed into bed with the same prayer drifting quite nervously from my tensed lips:

"God, show me if this Jesus is the Jewish Messiah and You want me to believe in Him." There was a battle being waged within and I experienced the anguish of every wounded soldier.

My sleep was sound and sweet. I woke at 6:00 A.M. and this time, instead of a radio, I heard a small, still voice speaking ever so delicately to me but with authoritative firmness:

"Vera, you go by the truth I have shown you and forget all your objections. Your parents, your friends, all the things you have put in the way, I'll take care of those. Just believe. Believe what I have shown you."

*July 1, 1962.* As a sheep would run to its shepherd, I spiritually ran to mine. He broke through the barriers of doubt and tradition and joyfully I yielded my life to Him. To my Jesus. To my Messiah.

# CHAPTER EIGHTEEN

# Completed!

I left my room and found Lisa. Greeting her for the first time as a sister in the Lord, I wrapped my arm around her shoulder.

"I'm one of you now."

Milton had already gone to the church to prepare for the Sunday morning service. Later, when the congregation had been seated, he announced we would be having communion, carefully explaining it should be taken only by those who have personally accepted Christ. I took it.

After the service I let all the others file past Milton and shake his hand while I hesitated near a pew. When the church was almost empty I approached him, feeling it took a minister to clinch the transaction!

"I'm ready."

"You are?"

"Yes, I am!"

"Where do you want to pray? Here or at home?"

"I don't care!"

We sat down in an apparently deserted church. Milton began to show me more Scripture (Romans 3:23; 6:23; John 1:12; Revelation 3:20). Why do I have to go through all this? Let's get on with it! I had already been convinced by the Bible, prayer and God's confirmation.

"Do you want to receive Christ?"

"Yes!"

I had actually accepted the Lord the moment I first believed, but did follow Milton's lead in thanking God for forgiving my sins through the sacrifice of the Messiah and then once again claimed the Life which was already mine.

The only sins I was aware of which I had committed were not keeping the Sabbath or the dietary laws. In my excitement I had forgotten it was because of the fact that neither I, nor anyone else, could ever keep every law as dictated in the Old Testament; that Jesus had to shed His blood as the final Passover lamb.

I felt numb. Absolutely numb. Years of struggling and searching as I experienced the wrath of man and patience of God had finally led me to the Lord's grace.

An hour or two later the numbness was replaced with an inner peace and bubbling joy which was literally from out of this world! Then I realized I hadn't changed my religion, I hadn't converted. I had simply become completed. I had recognized and believed in the promised Messiah, who came once to die for our sin and will come again soon to reign in His place as an eternal King in Israel!

I felt right at home when the church members hugged me and welcomed me as another who had come by faith. I told them I wanted to join their church, even though I didn't know what this entailed.

About two months later when Lisa was driving me back to the city, we sang "How Great Thou Art" again as well as "Living for Jesus." Now that I could tap an endless love from the Lord, Lisa mentioned something which stabbed me in the innermost part of my heart. She inquired about my attitude toward Germans:

In the past people were always trying to introduce me to my countrymen but I never cared to meet them. I didn't consider myself a German, nor did I have a German citizenship. Each time I met a German I wanted him to prove himself to me. Those my age who pleaded ignorance of the atrocities which had occurred were very defensive and very evasive. I did my best to avoid contact with them.

Lisa said my attitude wasn't pleasing to the Lord. She said vengeance belongs to God, not us, and we are to allow Him to love others through us instead of hating them because of what they had done.

So, just before attending High Holy Day services with my parents I dropped to my knees and, with great effort, asked the Lord to take away this deeply ingrained hatred I felt for Germans. I felt more of a burden lifted then than when I first accepted the Lord! My generation may be poisoned with spiritual blindness, but the hatred I had felt was replaced with love and concern. God knows. Only He could do that.

Marga, the first to know, nearly exploded. She wasn't so much upset that my beliefs had changed, she really didn't care. But she was furious that now I would become a bigot and not identify with the Jewish people anymore. I was horrified. Was this her concept of Christianity? Yet I couldn't complain, for we had shared similar feelings until I began asking God what *He* thought.

This was two weeks after my decision. Marga tried to make me promise I would either tell my parents while she was still in Los Angeles on a visit or not tell them at all.

I didn't want Marga's opposition when I told them, for although I was positive I had done the right thing my explanations might waver under a constant attack. Yet—I couldn't promise I wouldn't tell them. It's hard to keep quiet about a divine heart transplant.

I said nothing. After taking Marga to the train on a Friday so she could head back for Texas I dropped my parents at the bus stop. I thought we would have fifteen to twenty minutes before the bus came. I was to leave in my car at once for a weekend at the lake.

I planned to tell them what had transpired while we waited for the bus. Two New Testaments, prophecy editions, burned in my purse and I feared they'd see the smoke! I wanted to hand them the Bibles and pull a quick hit-and-run, explaining we would discuss everything when I returned.

The bus came at once. Father was boarding the bus just as mother hesitated to say good-bye.

"Here, I have these, I want you to read them. We'll talk when I come down from the lake! Bye!"

It may have been a rather crude method of telling them but there was no good way. Nothing would have been smooth. I worried the entire time. Could father have had a heart attack on the way home? He was already two years past the limit set by the Texas physician.

I was really chicken when I called them Saturday night. I told the operator to tell me when the three minutes were up! Father wasn't home but mother started in after we exchanged a few opening hellos.

"What do you mean by what you gave us?"

"I believe it and I want you to read it too."

"Did you join the church?"

"That's not the point. I believe that . . ."

"Did you join the church?"

". . . that Jesus is the Messiah."

*"But did you join the church?"*

"Mother, the main thing is that I believe Jesus is my Saviour."

"But did you . . . ?"

"Three minutes!"

"Thank you, operator. OK, mother, good-bye!"

Whew. Not understanding, I would have been upset too. Father came home and called me back, not letting me get away with a three-minute time limit. After the same questions father said he wanted to talk to Mr. Palmer.

"I'm sure he would like to talk to you," I said

calmly, "but he isn't home. Would you like him to call you back?"

Father said yes, then made one more comment about my belief before hanging up. "If you want me to die, you go right ahead."

My hand still rested on the phone as a young couple entered the Palmers' home and were bouncing with the enthusiasm of any young couple who had just gotten engaged. The girl showed me a gorgeous ring. I nodded, "That's nice." My apathy must have shocked them! They were looking for Lisa and I asked them to send her right home if they found her at church.

Lisa came immediately and we prayed. This was the first real experience I had with praying to my personal, loving Jesus. It's as if I stepped from a chilly night into a heated pool full of God's serenity, the peace gradually inching up my body until I was swimming in a divine quietness.

The fireworks erupted on Monday when Milton confronted my parents in Los Angeles. They accused him and said it was all his fault I had made this terrible decision. Milton, laughing in a very kindly way, said, "That's my business!"

"You make it a business!"

Father and mother completely missed the point and never let me live it down. Needless to say relations were not the best between my parents and Milton. They insisted on talking to me again, so the Palmers drove me to the city on Tuesday and came back Wednesday to pick me up. I was going to stay at the lake for a week.

I tried to explain to my parents. No luck.

After this hectic month of July, I was summoned to San Antonio by Marga. To talk with our old rabbi. I complied with her wishes, and Eric led off upon my arrival by asking: "Do you remember what I told you twenty years ago?"

"No, what?"

"Obviously you can't remember what I said twenty years ago. How did the disciples remember what to write down in the Bible?"

I admit he took me off guard but I countered by explaining I remembered our rabbi's sermon in Amsterdam about loving God. That was sixteen years before. Besides, the rabbi wasn't Jesus. If I had been with the Messiah during his three-year ministry I would have remembered every word He said.

So then I went to see the rabbi.

My former spiritual leader referred to Marilyn Monroe, implying I was a lonely mixed-up female who needed a crutch. He put it rather badly. Then he tried to hit me hard.

"Do you take the Bible literally?"

"Yes, I do."

"You can't do that."

"We have no grounds for discussion then. I always have."

The rabbi threatened me with rejection by my Jewish family, friends and Israel. He reached his logical conclusion.

"Don't you think you need a psychiatrist?"

"No."

"I think you do. Let me check with a friend."

He thumbed through some numbers, picked up the phone and called his friend. The rabbi explained about the woman who was with him and would the psychiatrist, at home on a Saturday afternoon, possibly have any free time? He would? How marvelous!

What a setup! He stood, pulled the drapes, and suggested I rest. He could see I was very tired and shut the door after him.

I made use of the plush rug by once more kneeling and committing everything to the Lord. He responded in typical fashion with His promised peace beyond human understanding.

"Why do you hate your parents?" the psychiatrist began. "Why did you have to tell them? Other Jewish people go to church, but why did you tell them? Why do you hate them?"

Umph. It never occurred to me *not* to tell them. How could I live a lie? I told them because I was happy I had made a decision and thought I was the only Jew who had ever done that!

The psychiatrist told me there was nothing wrong, yet Marga was extremely upset the day I left. She said the psychiatrist had told the rabbi I really needed help and made me promise to follow through on the suggestion I get help when I returned to California. I promised.

I knew my decision wasn't based on a psychiatric problem, but as a doctor I also knew the patient doesn't always know. The Palmers sent me to a Christian psychiatrist. When he had heard my story he broke out laughing, explaining this was a common happening when some persons changed their faith and he said some new believers are even committed to institutions by their families!

Without worrying, he said if my family persisted in

their demands I should take some tests to have evidence of my sanity in black and white. They did—and I did. The tests showed me to be perfectly sane, happy and peaceful.

Marga didn't believe it. The change they saw in me must have some answer, so they concluded I was crazy. What else? Too bad they were unfamiliar with the simplicity of accepting the Messiah, for the apostle Paul, a great Jewish leader and bold persecutor of Christians before God called him, declared, "I am crucified with Christ: nevertheless I live; yet not I, but Christ liveth in me: and the life which I now live in the flesh I live by the faith of the Son of God, who loved me, and gave himself for me" (Galatians 2:20).

No wonder I was different! It's a shame that most believers don't appropriate what is already theirs. Mother kept persisting in her original diagnosis until I said I had gone along with her as much as possible and it was of no use for her to continue. She stopped.

*September 22, 1962.* Just before the High Holidays. Milton baptized me as my sign of obedience to the Lord and to publicly acclaim the faith which I already possessed. Jesus commanded His disciples to be baptized. Not for salvation. Not for another dose of grace. But as a symbol of what had developed beyond the eyes of man: the invasion of His love into the heart.

October 1962. Father became deathly ill. I saw him at the hospital and he had a tube from every opening, his consciousness fading quickly. What should I do, Lord? Stay with him or go to the lake and pray?

Wednesday I drove to the lake for a prayer meeting and came back to the hospital on Thursday. Father was sitting up in bed! No tubes. Ready to go home. Amazing!

It was time for me to fly to Chicago to take the oral examination for my pediatric board certification, the second part of the test I had begun in January with a written exam.

I had wanted to arrive a few days early and do a little cramming but stayed with father. I went to Chicago the night before the test.

Through the years I always did well on written exams and blanked out during oral cross fire. Even when I went on ward rounds in the hospital my mind was erased and I froze in my tracks when the doctor asked me a question.

I kept praying the Lord would hold my hand and give me recall. I knew the material but needed to pry it loose when needed. Hold my hand, Lord, hold my hand.

I was the calmest of twelve doctors taking the test. One at a time we subjected ourselves to two hours of questions, placing ourselves before one doctor after another. My family had bet against me passing, thinking my faith would eliminate my love of medicine.

I made it! Or, should I say, Someone plucked out the information for me!

During the following years I became firmly grafted into the Tree of Life and was astounded at the fruit He could bear on His branches if we would just surrender and let Him work through us! Too often I would meet people who tried to help out poor little

God. Poor little God brought me life and fulfilled my Judaism! He didn't need help.

Some of my Jewish friends think I cannot be Jewish and Christian at the same time. I can understand their reasoning, for I thought the same way only a few short years ago. But the Bible speaks about three groups of people: Jews, gentiles and Christians. We have nothing to do with our birth—we are either Jews or gentiles, but then each individual can by faith allow the Messiah (Christ) to take over his or her life. In that way you become a follower of Christ, or a Christian.

The New Testament calls this a new birth, or a spiritual birth (John 3). Although I have always strongly identified with my Jewish people, I can say without reservation that I feel even more Jewish since I accepted Jesus as my Messiah.

Father, sick from time to time during the years, became critically ill in July of 1969. His doctor said his only chance was to successfully receive a pacemaker for his heart, a real last-ditch measure. I was in San Antonio, nursing Marga who was very sick herself. I would sit on her bed and we'd hold hands, talking about life, death and, as often as possible, eternity. I flew back to Los Angeles. At 7:00 A.M. I stood by father's bed, watching him slowly pass out before my eyes after receiving a pre-operative shot. He stopped breathing.

Am I imagining this? Even as a doctor it's hard to be objective with your own father. I quickly prayed and received the Lord's peace. I couldn't interpret the peace. Either father would pull through or else, if he died, he would be with the Lord.

At the moment he stopped breathing a nurse came in, took one look and yelled for the doctor. A surgeon came, got rattled and told mother he was dying, and then mother became shook up.

Father, shaking and barely breathing, was almost gone. The surgeon turned to mother and said, "Don't tell me you've been here the past two weeks and seen him go downhill and now act like it's such a big surprise that he's dying!"

They wheeled him into the operating room at 8:30 A.M., saying it would take them a half-hour to give him a pacemaker. I knew they would have to get him ready so figured it would take at least until 10:00 A.M. Plenty of time.

Ten o'clock came. Nothing. Ten-thirty. No word. Then eleven came—eleven-thirty.

I kept calling my office, telling my nurse I didn't know what was happening and father may well be gone by now. I thought he had died on the operating table and they were still trying a few desperate measures to revive him.

The peace never left me. At noon the cardiologist said they tried for three hours to get his heart to accept the catheter but it wouldn't latch on to it.

They sewed him back up, the last-ditch measure a failure, and father lived on without it!

# CHAPTER NINETEEN

# Confident of This Very Thing

Marga died on February 27, 1970. During the time I spent with her before her death I saw a frozen heart melt under the warmth of God's message. The Lord gave me an assurance she was with Him.

We thought father would never survive the shock of Marga's death but he did. Four months later a man knocked him over as he was walking on the street, just punched him to the ground for no reason, and he was bedridden for months. Father, at seventy-nine, had lost blood internally and bruised his hip.

I would often talk to him about the Lord, fearing his death was imminent and I wanted to be sure he accepted eternal life for his soul. This time I asked him about making a decision.

"I wish I could, but I can't. It's too late, I can't think anymore."

I told him many people missed out on the Lord's grace by thinking their way into confusion. All he needed to do was let go of himself and give in to God, telling Him he wanted to come His way. It's faith, but not blind faith. The Light of the world doesn't shed darkness on His children.

*January 3, 1971.* He went back to the hospital.

I knew this time it was going to be it. I didn't mention the Lord for a while since it had to be his decision. God is a perfect gentleman. He'll never twist your arm to force you to believe. He'll just keep waiting—and loving. One day father held my hand.

"Now I know why Marga always wanted you around. When you're here I feel such a peace."

"That's because when I'm here the Lord is too!"
He smiled.

A nun at the hospital, the chaplain's assistant, said she'd pray with father and he really loved it. Father concurred. "She prayed with me and didn't use any name or anything. It was really nice." I knew I had to talk to the nun.

On a Sunday he said how concerned he was for me but I assured him his concern didn't match mine for him. I told father I was still expecting to hear good news from him. He knew what I meant from many other conversations I'd had with him.

"Well, let me tell you," father said, barely able to talk, "I'm eighty years old, brought up in this religion and I can't change now."

I told him eighty years is nothing when compared to forever, and besides, he *wasn't* changing religions, just accepting his Messiah.

Father said he had heard two Messiahs were coming. I asked him where, in Judaism or Christianity? In either case he was wrong. Jewish elders, unable to reconcile a suffering Messiah with a kingly Messiah as being one person, had traditionally and not biblically come up with two persons. Then Old Testament prophecies of the suffering Messiah were gradually ignored and faded into nothing.

I explained Yom Kippur, the Day of Atonement, offered a covering, or covering over of our sins (the meaning of the word "kippur"). It took the Lamb of God, the Messiah, the only perfect, acceptable sacrifice to wash our sins away forever.

God, in all His love, allowed the blood of His only Son to be shed because every man on earth had fallen short of His glory.

We are all slaves to sin, both by nature and deed, and only a free man can buy freedom for a slave. Jesus, the only one free of sin, was the only one able to purchase us. "Grant us redemption," the Orthodox prayer book cried out, "redeem us."

"I think you believe all that, don't you, father?"

He nodded. I hugged him and told him he would be all right.

On Wednesday, Doug Pyle, a gentile who behaves as if he was raised on chicken soup and bagels and loves Jewish people more than most Jews, came to visit father.

Doug's ministry is to bring Old Testament promises and prophecies alive to Jewish people and let God show how they lead to Jesus. Being extremely sensitive to the Lord's Spirit, Doug always has a heavy burden when asked to visit unbelievers. He didn't feel this with father. Doug's mother, a licensed vocational nurse, had visited my parents before. That afternoon mother asked for Mrs. Pyle to visit. I was thrilled!

During the days of waiting for father to pass away I prayed I would be with mother when he finally went. The ordeal had tired me so a friend was driving me all over Los Angeles from the hospital, to my office, apartment, back to the hospital and so on.

When I saw Mrs. Pyle at the hospital she said she had good news for me. I knew what she meant. Father was happy to see her and she wasted no time in telling him he needed the Messiah to go to heaven. He smiled and squeezed her hand. Then she explained the blood of the Messiah is the atonement for our sins. He nodded again.

That morning I saw the nun, asking her to pray in Jesus' name when she was with father since I was concerned for his salvation. He had already heard the gospel and wouldn't be offended.

She agreed, found a nice prayer in her book which mentioned salvation and the prince of peace and read it to father.

"In Jesus' name?" she concluded.

He grinned and tightened his grip on her fingers.

That afternoon he could only say, "Meta, Meta," my mother's name, over and over again. I straightened his pillow and he turned to me.

". . . you did . . . it."

"The right thing?"

"Yes."

I stayed with mother at her apartment. The next morning I called the hospital at four o'clock and found out father was worse. I couldn't rush mother, fearing she would panic. We'd leave when the Lord was ready.

I had a feeling we should be there by 6:00 A.M., but we didn't leave the apartment until that time. We arrived at 6:20 A.M.

*January 29, 1971.* Father had died at five minutes to six. If they had called us and said he was gone it would have been much harder.

I have the peace, the assurance, the knowledge that I'll see Charltje, father and Marga again in the presence of the Lord! And for the first time I'll meet my sister who never grew up in our world!

When I believed on Jesus as my Messiah I thought I had been the first Jew to do this. Was I wrong! Ever since our Jewish fathers became the Lord's disciples, formed the early Christian church and began to witness to the gentiles there has always been a remnant of Jews who were true believers. Even back in Elijah's time the prophet thought he stood alone in worshiping God until the Lord pointed out seven thousand others!

Across America there are increasing numbers of Hebrew Christians, living testimony to the prophecy: "Afterward shall the children of Israel return, and seek the LORD their God, and David their king; and shall fear the LORD and his goodness in the latter days" (Hosea 3:5).

What are the latter days? Right now—while the prophecies in Daniel, Ezekiel, Zechariah, Matthew and other portions of Scripture are being fulfilled!

When Jesus preached to the Jews thousands believed, but those in positions of great authority, like the Pharisees, usually considered Him only as a threat to their status. As a completed Jew I cherish how my Messiah answered them:

"I told you, and ye believed not: the works that I do in my Father's name, they bear witness of me. But ye believe not, because ye are not of my sheep, as I said unto you. My sheep hear my voice, and I know them, and they follow me: And I give unto them eternal life; and they shall never perish, neither shall any *man* pluck them out of my hand. . . . I and my Father are one" (John 10:25-28,30).

The evidences of a crumbling world surround us in the forms of increased crime, death by mind-bending drugs and an epidemic of emptiness felt by paupers and wealthy alike.

What's missing?

Perfection! The Messiah's perfection. The kind which man constantly strives for but can never achieve. The kind that only Jesus can bring to an empty human heart.

We don't have to wait until physical death to discover whether the Lord exists or not! He's dynamic and alive and will move in our lives if we let Him. Yet the daily excitement I feel from knowing my

Messiah now can't compare with how I'll feel when He returns!

Over three hundred prophecies in the Old Testament discuss our Lord's first advent which occurred almost two thousand years ago, but the Old Testament also contains over five hundred references to the Second Coming! Can you imagine sitting at the same table with Abraham, Isaac and Jacob in God's kingdom?

Jesus said we must be *born again*. To Nicodemus, a leader of the Jews, such an idea was fantastic. "Can a man climb into his mother's womb and be born again?" he asked. Jesus answered, "Except a man be born of water *and* of the Spirit, he cannot enter into the kingdom of God." Also, the apostle Peter says, "Being born again, not of corruptible seed, but of incorruptible, by the word of God, which liveth and abideth forever" (1 Peter 1:23).

People ask me how I, as a doctor, could believe as I do. How, as a doctor, can I not believe? All you have to do is see how perfectly a newborn human being comes from a microscopic egg. A quirk of fate? A mere accident? That's fantastic! There is no conflict between science and God!

As I think back to the agony of my youth, the torture, hunger and anxiety of the concentration camp and the way I fought against my God when He desired to show me a greater truth, I can only praise His name for His grace and thank Him for His Word:

"Being confident of this very thing, that he which hath begun a good work in you will perform *it* until the day of Jesus Christ" (Philippians 1:6). The day I accepted Christ Pastor Palmer gave me this verse. How true! He began a work in me a long time ago, and He is still working!

"And we know that all things work together for good to them that love God, to them who are the called according to *his* purpose" (Romans 8:28).

*Gam zeletauvo!*